Maker Innovations Series

Jump start your path to discovery with the Apress Maker Innovations series! From the basics of electricity and components through to the most advanced options in robotics and Machine Learning, you'll forge a path to building ingenious hardware and controlling it with cutting-edge software. All while gaining new skills and experience with common toolsets you can take to new projects or even into a whole new career.

The Apress Maker Innovations series offers projects-based learning, while keeping theory and best processes front and center. So you get hands-on experience while also learning the terms of the trade and how entrepreneurs, inventors, and engineers think through creating and executing hardware projects. You can learn to design circuits, program AI, create IoT systems for your home or even city, and so much more!

Whether you're a beginning hobbyist or a seasoned entrepreneur working out of your basement or garage, you'll scale up your skillset to become a hardware design and engineering pro. And often using low-cost and open-source software such as the Raspberry Pi, Arduino, PIC microcontroller, and Robot Operating System (ROS). Programmers and software engineers have great opportunities to learn, too, as many projects and control environments are based in popular languages and operating systems, such as Python and Linux.

If you want to build a robot, set up a smart home, tackle assembling a weather-ready meteorology system, or create a brand-new circuit using breadboards and circuit design software, this series has all that and more! Written by creative and seasoned Makers, every book in the series tackles both tested and leading-edge approaches and technologies for bringing your visions and projects to life.

More information about this series at https://link.springer.com/bookseries/17311

Git for Electronic Circuit Design

CAD and Version Control for Electrical Engineers

Altay Brusan
Aytac Durmaz

Apress®

Git for Electronic Circuit Design: CAD and Version Control for Electrical Engineers

Altay Brusan, PhD
Bogazici University,
Istanbul, Turkey

Aytac Durmaz, PhD
Bogazici University,
Istanbul, Turkey

ISBN-13 (pbk): 978-1-4842-8123-9
https://doi.org/10.1007/978-1-4842-8124-6

ISBN-13 (electronic): 978-1-4842-8124-6

Managing Director, Apress Media LLC: Welmoed Spahr
Acquisitions Editor: Aaron Black
Development Editor: James Markham
Coordinating Editor: Jessica Vakili

Cover designed by eStudioCalamar

Cover image designed by Freepik (www.freepik.com)

Distributed to the book trade worldwide by Springer Science+Business Media New York, 1 New York Plaza, Suite 4600, New York, NY 10004-1562, USA. Phone 1-800-SPRINGER, fax (201) 348-4505, e-mail orders-ny@springer-sbm.com, or visit www.springeronline.com. Apress Media, LLC is a California LLC and the sole member (owner) is Springer Science + Business Media Finance Inc (SSBM Finance Inc). SSBM Finance Inc is a **Delaware** corporation.

For information on translations, please e-mail booktranslations@springernature.com; for reprint, paperback, or audio rights, please e-mail bookpermissions@springernature.com.

Apress titles may be purchased in bulk for academic, corporate, or promotional use. eBook versions and licenses are also available for most titles. For more information, reference our Print and eBook Bulk Sales web page at http://www.apress.com/bulk-sales.

Any source code or other supplementary material referenced by the author in this book is available to readers on GitHub via the book's product page, located at www.apress.com/ 978-1-4842-8123-9. For more detailed information, please visit http://www.apress.com/ source-code.

Printed on acid-free paper

In memory of H. Brusan

Table of Contents

About the Authors...xi

About the Technical Reviewer xiii

Acknowledgments xv

Introduction xvii

Chapter 1: Basics...1

Introduction...1

Initializing a Repository on a Microsoft Windows Environment 3

Using a Repository 6

Look Inside the Stage Area 12

Delete a File 14

Rename and Relocate a File 16

Ignore a File 19

Inside a Repository 23

Log History...27

Peek into an Entity...32

Inside the Local Repository and Stage Area...33

Comparing...35

How Does Git Compare?...35

How to Compare? 40

Restore...44

Reset...48

Revert Without Conflict 54

Get Files Out of a Commit 57

Clean Untracked Files 59

Summary 60

Chapter 2: Branches 63

Overview 63

Creating Branches 66

Change the Active Branch 67

Change the Branch Name 72

Delete a Branch 72

Compare Branches 74

Stash 76

Move on a Branch 78

Merge Branches 80

    Fast-Forward Merge 80

    Three-Way Merge 84

Merge Flowchart 91

    How to Configure Microsoft Visual Studio Code as the
    Default Merging Tool 92

Squash Merge 96

Rebasing 100

Cherry-Pick 106

Cancel a Merge 109

    Revert with Conflicts 111

Restore 116

Tag 117

Summary 118

Chapter 3: Remote Repository 121

Create a Repository in GitHub 122

Clone a Remote Repository...124

Push, Fetch, Pull Commands...126

Remote Connections 139

Race Condition 148

Tags and Releases 153

Merge Independent Repositories 156

Fork..159

Summary..162

Chapter 4: Commit Reforming 165

Reflog Command...166

Garbage Collection..168

Amend the Last Commit..170

Amend a Middle Commit...173

Rewording a Commit Message 177

Change the Commit Order...178

Combine Commits..180

Summary..181

Chapter 5: Managing a Circuit Design Project...............................183

Workspace Template..184

Project Development Workflow 192

Documentation..195

Iteration Plan 196

Risk Plan...198

Version Control of an Electronic Project......................................200

Summary..202

Chapter 6: Application 203

Case Study: SyncBox 203

Step 1: Requirement Analysis...205

Step 2: System Analysis 209

Step 3: System Design..212

Step 4: Implementation 216

Step 5: Release...223

Altium Designer and Git...224

Case Study: RPi COM 4 Extension Board...227

Summary...234

Correction to: Git for Electronic Circuit Design................................. C1

Index...235

About the Authors

Altay Brusan has academic and field experience as a software engineer and digital circuit designer. He has developed open source and commercial projects in medical applications, such as iBEX software for radiology workstations and medical imaging hardware platforms. Altay is eager to share his 10 years of experience to help electronics engineers with less of a software background understand Git.

Aytac Durmaz received his BS in electrical and electronics engineering from Bilkent University in 2007 and both his MSc (2010) and PhD in biomedical engineering (2019) from Boğaziçi University. His current professional focus and researches are on IoT devices and platforms, software development, and medical devices. Durmaz is also the founder of several start-ups focused on medical devices, IoT, software development, and marine systems.

About the Technical Reviewer

 **Mezgani Ali** is a doctor in God sciences and religious studies and a PhD student of transmissions, telecommunications, and artificial intelligence (National Institute of Posts and Telecommunications in Rabat). He has a master's degree Research of Superior Institute of science and technologies (MPSI) Mathematics and Computer science in France, Laureate of classes of Engineer MPSI Degree in Morocco (My Youssef High School, Rabat).

Mezgani has worked for NIC France, Capgemini, HP, and Orange and was part of a team of site reliability engineers (SREs) responsible for keeping data center servers and customer applications up and running. He is fanatical about Kubernetes, REST API, MySQL, and Scala and is the creator of the functional and imperative programming language PASP. Mezgani's first program was a horoscope in BASIC in 1993 and since then has done extensive work on the infrastructure side in system engineering, software engineering, managed networks, and security.

He is a researcher at Native LABS, Inc.

Mezgani is technical reviewer of several book titles for Apress and in his spare time likes exploring technology, reading, and spending time with his young daughter, Ghita.

Acknowledgments

We are utterly grateful to Prof. Dr. Cengizhan Ozturk, who opened X-lab doors for curiosity, provided an excellent example for a nourishing future, and with his wisdom enlightened the room. We are grateful to Asuman Kolbasi for her great feedback and help in preparing the materials.

Altay Brusan is thoroughly thankful to Latifeh Gonbadi for her encouragement and affection in all aspects of his life. He appreciates and is grateful to his beautiful wife, Mahsa Modarresi, for her love, passion, support, and patience on this journey.

Introduction

Computer-Aided Design (CAD) tools have an essential role in modern-age engineering. Specifically, circuit design tools have been advanced and professionalized in recent years. These tools make the job, which is classically done using pen and paper, easy for engineers; however, CAD systems require a new development ecosystem. The *collaboration*, *sharing*, *backup*, and *management* phases in modern projects need special tools and methods. Luckily, the software engineering ecosystem is full of tools that have already proven their capacity. Among them is Git, which is a cornerstone of modern-age software development and has already been applied in mainstream projects, such as Linux development. In recent years, Git has found its way in CAD applications also. It has eased the way the team members share their work and provided a centralized backup system, and essentially, it provides the facility for team managers to monitor the progress. However, Git is a double-edged sword! Without an educated application, it could end up in total chaos or even project failure! For this reason, all newcomers or even seasoned engineers with no background in software engineering need to know Git.

What Is Inside?

Git has hundreds of commands with many parameters. Learning all of them is not practical and not required at all! In the first part of this book, we focus on the Git language essentials. However, the contents are prepared based on two mindsets.

The original version of this book was revised. A correction to this book is available at https://doi.org/10.1007/978-1-4842-8124-6_7

First, no graphical user interface (GUI) is sufficient. There are many free, open source, and commercial GUIs available for Git; however, in reality these tools are not a golden bullet for all scenarios. Based on an unwritten software engineering rule, if a chance of a bug is one in a billion, that problem would definitely happen one day! Same goes for the Git-based management system. In a shared environment, the chance of a collision and data loss is not negligible. Unfortunately, there are situations where we need to intervene and apply a chain of a complex set of commands to solve a conflict or problem. These kinds of scenarios are not usually available in a GUI.

The other way is to keep stuff as simple as possible and follow a consistent streamlined method. In the first part of the book, from Chapters 1 to 4, the only focus point is on Git itself. Chapter 1 introduces fundamentals of Git-more specifically the "commit." We can imagine a commit as a single brick that stores a snapshot of history. In Chapter 2, we learn how to organize commits in a special chain of history lines (named branches). Metaphorically, in this chapter, we will learn how to make a wall out of bricks! In Chapter 3, we learn how to use a complete version control system. In other words, we make a decorated house out of the walls, and finally in Chapter 4, we will learn how to trim the house for a better facad. In the first four chapters, the focus is only on Git syntax and how Git works underneath. To keep the materials simple, instead of schematics or PCB files, we use plain-text files to study Git behavior and compare the outputs more easily. Then, we get into the second part of the book: Git and CAD! In Chapter 5, we are introduced to Git's best practices, project organization and how to structure the materials, and project management methods. These guidelines are prepared based on years of experience in the field and could save lives for start-ups. Finally, in Chapter 6, this knowledge is applied by developing two open source hardware design projects, and we will see Git in action.

CHAPTER 1

Basics

This book introduces Git from the eyes of a circuit designer. In this chapter, we will see the basics of Git through hands-on exercises and discuss concepts through examples in the command-line environment. This will help you to interactively learn the concept.

Introduction

Git is a free and open source tool for tracking changes, sharing documents, preparing backups, and collaboration between team members.

Git was initially created by Linus Torvalds for Linux kernel development. It is primarily developed for Linux, but it has been extended to be used on other Unix operating systems including BSD, Solaris, and Darwin. Git is extremely fast on POSIX-based systems such as Linux. It differs from other version control systems such as Apache SVN such that it creates a private repository on a remote server too. Recently, Git has found its way in Computer-Aided Design (CAD) software; specifically, Altium Designer was a pioneer in this regard.

By shifting CAD technology toward Git, it is now a necessity for electronic circuit designers to understand Git. Git automatically installs its default terminal, which is named git bash (Figure 1-1). In this terminal, we can execute Git commands. Additionally, this environment emulates Linux terminals and provides the facility for executing basic Linux commands such as creating (touch), removing (rm), and renaming (mv) files and directories (e.g., mkdir).

© Altay Brusan and Aytac Durmaz 2022
A. Brusan and A. Durmaz, *Git for Electronic Circuit Design*, Maker Innovations Series,
https://doi.org/10.1007/978-1-4842-8124-6_1

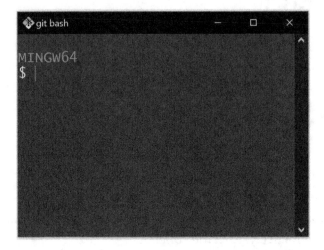

Figure 1-1. *The Bash console is automatically installed by Git*

Note   Git does not require a graphical user interface (GUI). There are free and commercial user interfaces available. However, in complex scenarios, the UI packages do not magically solve or avoid a chaotic circumstance. For this reason, a concrete understanding about Git is very useful. The best way to solidify the concepts is through practicing the Git commands. You should practice each command on your machine.

A Git command has special semantics:

`git + command + parameters`

It starts with the git keyword, then the command name follows, and then parameters come after. All Git commands are documented. To read the document related to a command, we can use the `--help` parameter, like

`$ git  init  --help`

Note   To increase readability and simplify the concepts, all examples in the first part of the book (Chapter 1 through Chapter 4) are based on text files. In the second part, circuit design using CAD systems is discussed, and examples are provided based on more realistic file formats.

Before starting Git, it's worth mentioning that Git follows the Linux file access convention. For example: "." stands for local directory and ".." parent directory, "*" means all, and directories are delimited by "/".

Initializing a Repository on a Microsoft Windows Environment

To start using Git, the first step is to initialize a repository. Move the current location to the place that the repository is going to be made, for example:

```
cd "D:\tutorial\git\Chapter-1"
```

The change directory (cd) command redirects the current location to the selected path (e.g., "D:\tutorial\git\Chapter-1"). Using the init command, we can initialize a repository inside this location. For example

```
git init demo01
```

creates a demo01 folder and initializes a Git repository inside it. demo01 is called a ***workspace***. The command output is

```
Initialized empty Git repository in D:/tutorial/git/Chapter-1/
demo01/.git/
```

We can check the content of demo01. Inside demo01, Git created a new hidden directory named .git (Figure 1-2), which handles all the magic inside. In this book, we will not get involved with the internals of this folder. It is enough to think that Git records all the changes that happen inside demo01 within the .git folder.

Figure 1-2. *The .git folder is automatically created by Git to track all changes made inside demo01*

Figure 1-3 shows the internal organization of a repository. Git monitors the contents of a workspace and stores the changes in two stages: in the first stage, Git detects changes that happen to files such as *create, update, delete,* or *move* and makes a list of all changed files; then, the user picks a subset (or all) of the items in the list and asks Git to add the selected files into the ***staging*** (also named indexing or cache) area. When a file is entered into the staging area, it is under the Git radar, and anytime any change happens to it, Git automatically notices and computes the differences with the previous copy. Nonetheless, the staging area is a temporary place. In this area only one copy of each file is kept. So only the most updated version of each file would override the previous one. For this reason, Git requires the second stage, which stores a snapshot of the files at each moment of time. In other words, in the second stage, Git encapsulates all (or a subset of files that the user wishes) from the staging area and stores them inside the local database. This database is called a local ***repository***.

Figure 1-3. *Git repository organization: The workspace is the directory in which the repository is made. The index/stage area is where the most updated forms of files are placed temporarily, and the local repository stores the history permanently*

Git is very efficient with using storage space. It applies efficient methods for compressing and avoiding repetitive copies of files. In Git files are stored as they are! Consider Figure 1-4. At (1) File1.txt and File2.txt are created in the workspace. Then they are staged (2) and finally stored in the local repository (3). Sometime later, only File1.txt is updated in the workspace (4) and staged (5). Now, if we ask Git to encapsulate all files inside the stage area and store them into the local repository, as File1.txt is changed, its updated version is saved into the local repository as is,[1] but File2.txt is not changed, so to save space Git creates a pointer to the previous copy of File2.txt. This pointer and updated copy of File1.txt are stored in the local repository (6). In this way, Git avoids replicating unmodified files and saves storage.

---

[1] Compared with other version control systems that only save changes that happened to the files.

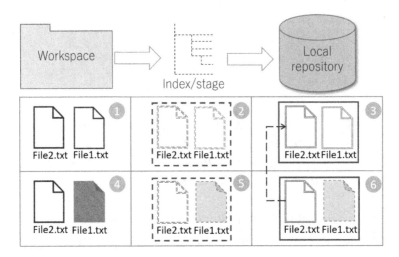

Figure 1-4. *(1) File1.txt and File2.txt are created, staged (2), and then stored in the local repository (3). File1.txt is updated (4) and then staged (5). The updated stage area contents are stored into the local repository (6). File1.txt is physically updated and a fresh copy is saved into local repository; however, File2.txt did not change, so a pointer to the previous copy is placed in the last commit-instead of replicating File2.txt*

Using a Repository

Inside the workspace, File1.txt and File2.txt are created. As a quick shortcut, we use the Linux touch command like

```
touch File1.txt File2.txt
```

Using the status command, we can check if Git detects new changes:

```
$ git status
```

A snippet of the output is

Untracked files:
```
  (use "git add <file>..." to include in what will be committed)
    File1.txt
    File2.txt

nothing added to commit but untracked files present (use "git
add" to track)
```

These files are the first detected by Git. So they are categorized as untracked files. In the first step, we need to add them into the stage area using the add command:

```
$ git add File1.txt
$ git add File2.txt
```

It can also be done in one command:

```
$ git add .
```

Note   Git does not consider empty folders. To capture Git's attention to consider a folder, you need to add at least one file inside it.

From this point, File1.txt and File2.txt are inserted into the stage area. We can check this using the status command:

```
$ git status
Changes to be committed:
  (use "git rm --cached <file>..." to unstage)
    new file:   File1.txt
    new file:   File2.txt
```

Making new changes to files and adding them to the stage area overwrites the already existing copies. To finish the backup, files are required to be inserted into the local repository. This is done by the commit command:

```
$ git commit -m "File1.txt and File2.txt added"
```

The string after parameter m is a message that clarifies what happens inside this commit. When a series of commits are collected, these messages are useful to remember what happened inside the commits. So it is important to label commits with a meaningful message. The output of the commit is

```
[master (root-commit) e600fc0] File1.txt and File2.txt added
 2 files changed, 0 insertions(+), 0 deletions(-)
 create mode 100644 File1.txt
 create mode 100644 File2.txt
```

After the commit, the latest copy of all files inside the stage area is stored in the repository. Checking with git status confirms this:

```
$ git status
On branch master
nothing to commit, working tree clean
```

The -m parameter of the commit command receives a short title string (maximum of 80 characters). For a complete message, which includes both title and a long description, the -m parameter is not needed:

```
$ git commit
```

This command opens the Vim editor (a Linux-based text editor, which is Git's default text editor). The first line is the commit title, and then it is followed by a blank line. After the blank line, a long description could be added to the commit. The Vim editor may not be convenient for people outside of the Linux world. Fortunately, Git does not strictly depend on Vim, and it could be replaced by another editor. In the following chapters, we will see how to change the default editor to other graphical text editors.

Suppose Line1 is added into `File1.txt` (Figure 1-5).

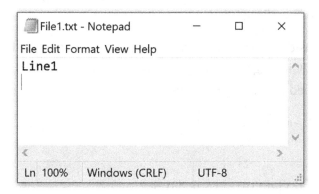

Figure 1-5. *File1.txt is updated*

If we check the status of the local repository

```
$ git status
```

```
On branch master
```

Changes not staged for commit:
```
  (use "git add <file>..." to update what will be committed)
  (use "git restore <file>..." to discard changes in working
  directory)
    modified:   File1.txt
```

```
no changes added to commit (use "git add" and/or "git
commit -a")
```

File1.txt already exists inside the stage area, but the copy inside the workspace is different from the staged one. So Git suggests adding the new version of File1.txt into the stage area. After accepting this suggestion

```
$ git add File1.txt
$ git status
```

Changes to be committed:
```
  (use "git restore --staged <file>..." to unstage)
    modified:   File1.txt
```

File1.txt inside the stage area is updated, but it is not stored in the local repository yet. Git suggests storing the updates inside the local repository. For this, we need to commit changes:

```
$ git commit -m "File1.txt updated"
```

the outputs

```
[master 86ef321] File1.txt updated
 1 file changed, 1 insertion(+)
```

We can select specific files to be included within a commit. Suppose File3.txt is created inside the foo directory and both File1.txt and File2.txt were updated. Then, all the changes are added into the stage area:

```
$ git add .
$ git status
```

```
Changes to be committed:
  (use "git restore --staged <file>..." to unstage)
    modified:   File1.txt
    modified:   File2.txt
    new file:   foo/File3.txt
```

Let's say we need to commit File1.txt and File2.txt in the first commit and another commit includes only File3.txt:

```
$ git commit -m "File1.txt File2.txt updated" File1.txt
File2.txt
$ git status
```

You should notice that file names come after the message and they are separated by a space. The output is

```
[master b48ef7b] File1.txt File2.txt updated
 2 files changed, 3 insertions(+)
```

Changes to be committed:
```
  (use "git restore --staged <file>..." to unstage)
    new file:   foo/File3.txt
```

Let's commit File3.txt:

```
$ git commit -m "File3.txt created" ./foo/File3.txt
```

```
[master 1135513] File3.txt created
 1 file changed, 0 insertions(+), 0 deletions(-)
 create mode 100644 foo/File3.txt
```

Git assigns a unique mode to each file that is committed in its repository. The file mode determines the execution permission. For regular files, it is equal to 100644, and for executable files, it is 100755.

To put it in a nutshell, changes are first *added* into the staging area and then *committed* into the local repository. This pattern is so common that a shortcut is available, which does both operations in a single run. The -a (all) parameter of the commit command enforces all modified files (does not include *untracked* files) to automatically be (re-)staged and committed into the local repository. A summary of common command flow is shown in Figure 1-6.

Note   The best practice is to separately stage files and then commit them into the local repository.

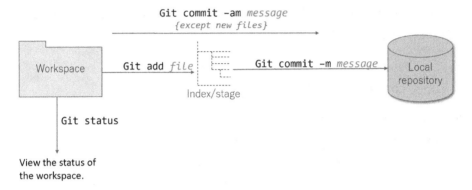

Figure 1-6. *Common commands used to transfer and store changes in different stages within the local repository*

Look Inside the Stage Area

Let's see the contents of the stage area:

```
$ git ls-files
```

```
File1.txt
File2.txt
foo/File3.txt
```

This information is good enough if we only need the files' names and their paths. However, we cannot take a look inside any files; for this we need the file's Id. In Git almost everything has a unique Id. Git uses the Id to uniquely identify the resource. We can use these Ids to directly access resources. Ids are generated by the SHA-1 hashing algorithm, and each one is a 40-character string, but most of the time the first five or seven characters are enough for Git to automatically figure out the remaining characters.

The ls-files command with the stage parameter provides a complete list of files and their Ids:

```
$ git ls-files --stage
```

```
100644 df714d8dc65c5b453d045b5fc6108b42b68175cf 0    File1.txt
100644 98a55606ee136b5d353abeb251a5a341033a4c9b 0    File2.txt
100644 e69de29bb2d1d6434b8b29ae775ad8c2e48c5391 0    foo/
                                                     File3.txt
```

In this report, the first number is the file mode. In this case, 100644 stands for non-executable files. The second string is the unique identifier of the file, and the last column is the file name. To see the contents of a specific file, we can use its Id, but instead of its complete Id number, we use the first five (or seven) characters. For example, let's see the File1.txt content inside the stage area:

```
$ git show df714
```

The output is File1.txt with Id df714:

```
Line1
Line2
```

The show command is a very handy tool. It discloses contents of a variety of Git entities. In this application we used the show command to see file contents. In the following, other applications of the show command are presented.

Once a file enters the stage area, it will stay there, and Git automatically takes an eye on its updates all the time. However, it may not be a behavior we are interested in. For example, a file may find its way into the stage area while it is not completed, or we may find that we do not need a file anymore and need Git to discard it. In these situations, we can inform Git to untrack a file. Suppose we have File1.txt, File2.txt, and File3.txt in our stage, like

```
File1.txt
File2.txt
foo/File3.txt
```

We want to remove File3.txt from the stage area. For this we can use the rm command with the --cache parameter:

```
$ git rm --cache ./foo/File3.txt
```

After this point, File3.txt is removed from the stage area.

Delete a File

Git repositories are sensitive, and their contents should be modified under Git supervision, specially deleting files. For example, if we delete a staged file like File1.txt from the workspace using the command line

```
rm File1.txt
```

the status of the repository will change as follows:

```
Changes not staged for commit:
  (use "git add/rm <file>..." to update what will be committed)
  (use "git restore <file>..." to discard changes in working
  directory)
      deleted:    File1.txt
```

Git noticed File1.txt was removed from the workspace; however, it is still in the stage list. We can check this with the ls-files command:

```
$ git ls-files
File1.txt
File2.txt
```

The deleted files are also required to be removed from the stage area. So, after deleting a file from the workspace, we need to add this change to the stage area and then commit it into the local repository:

```
$ git add  .
$ git status
$ git commit -m "File1.txt is deleted"
```

```
[master 8636b67] File1.txt deleted
 1 files changed, 3 deletions(-)
 delete mode 100644 File1.txt
```

Instead of removing a file from the workspace and stage area separately, Git has a remove command that deletes resources from both places at once. For example, suppose File1.txt and File2.txt are created and staged. To delete File1.txt from both the working directory and stage area, we use the git rm command like

```
$ git rm File1.txt
```

If the operation was successful, the output would be

```
rm 'File1.txt'
```

The remove command deletes a file from stage area and workspace. However, we still need to save this change in the local repository. We can check this with the status command:

```
$ git status
Changes to be committed:
  (use "git restore --staged <file>..." to unstage)
      deleted:    File1.txt

 1 file changed, 3 deletions(-)
 delete mode 100644 File1.txt
```

The rm command accepts regular expressions to ease file selection. For example, to delete all text files with the .txt extension, the "*.txt" string is useful, or to delete multiple files in one command, we can enlist the files' names with spaces in between them (e.g., git rm file1.txt file2.txt to remove file1.txt and file2.txt). To remove a directory with subdirectories and its contents, we can use recursive (-r) and forcefully (-f) parameters. For example, let's remove the foo directory with all its subdirectories and files:

```
$ git rm -rf foo
```

```
rm 'foo/File3.txt'
rm 'foo/bar/File5.txt'
rm 'foo/bar/File6.txt'
rm 'foo/bar/File7.txt'
```

Rename and Relocate a File

In Git, renaming a file is the same as relocating it. Indeed, each renaming is a relocation operation that happens inside the same directory. For this reason, both operations are done with the move (mv) command. The steps to use the git mv command are as follows:

1. Rename/relocate the target file inside the workspace.

2. Add the changes to the stage area.

3. Commit into the local repository content.

The move (mv) command needs two parameters: the first one is a path to the source file, and the second parameter is the *destination* file.

Suppose a typo in the file name happened and instead of File3.txt, Fil3.txt was created. To correct this, we can use

```
$ git mv Fil3.txt File3.txt
```

The output of the command is

```
(use "git restore --staged <file>..." to unstage)
    renamed:    Fil3.txt -> File3.txt
```

Similarly, to move a file from one directory into another place, we can use the mv command with a full path (including the destination name) to the destination:

```
git mv File4.txt ./foo/File4.txt
```

The mv command does not automatically create the destination directory. You should already check if the destination path exists and is spelled correctly; otherwise, you would receive a "No such file or directory" error.

Note The mv command works only for files that are already staged. Trying to rename or relocate a file that does not exist in the stage area would raise a "fatal: not under version control" error.

We can move a directory with all its contents from one place into another one. For example, let's move the *foo* directory under the *bar* directory:

```
$ git mv foo ./bar/
```

The "./" in front of bar shows that the bar directory is in the current active directory level.

mv does not automatically create the destination directories. This limitation is a major handicap for situations where a directory has many subdirectories such that making them one by one at the destination would be a tedious job. In this case, we can use the Linux mv command, for example:

```
mv -f log/* doc/
```

This command moves forcefully all the contents of the log directory into doc. It creates directories that do not exist under the destination path. After moving the source files to the destination point, we can check out the results using the status command:

```
$ git status --short
```

```
 D log/core/core-1.txt
 D log/core/core-2.txt
 D log/peripherals/peripheral-1.txt
 D log/peripherals/peripheral-2.txt
 D log/plugins/plugins.txt
?? doc/
```

The D in front of the file's name indicates that the file is deleted, and ?? indicates that the doc directory is not tracked yet (is not available in the stage area). We need to add these changes into the stage area such that Git notices the files are renamed/relocated (not deleted):

```
$ git add .
```

```
Changes to be committed:
  (use "git restore --staged <file>..." to unstage)
        renamed:    log/core/core-1.txt -> doc/core/core-1.txt
        renamed:    log/core/core-2.txt -> doc/core/core-2.txt
        renamed:    log/peripherals/peripheral-1.txt -> doc/
                    peripherals/peripheral-1.txt
        renamed:    log/peripherals/peripheral-2.txt -> doc/
                    peripherals/peripheral-2.txt
        renamed:    log/plugins/plugins.txt -> doc/plugins/
                    plugins.txt
```

Ignore a File

Git is sensitive to all changes happening inside the workspace. However, sometimes we may not be interested in tracking some files or contents of a directory like temporary documents or log files. The gitignore feature lets us pass over unwished files.

To activate gitignore after initializing an empty repository, the list of all unnecessary directories and files are inserted inside a special text file. This file must have no name, and its extension must be .gitignore.[2] As soon as the file is committed into the local repository, Git notices that it received an ignore list, and using that, it evaluates and ignores new coming contents. A sample ignore file is shown in Figure 1-7. In this file temp.txt inside the temp folder and all contents of the log folder are ignored.

---

[2] In Microsoft Windows, you should use the "Save as" option and then for the "File Name" field type ".gitignore". Otherwise, Notepad automatically changes the file extension to .txt.

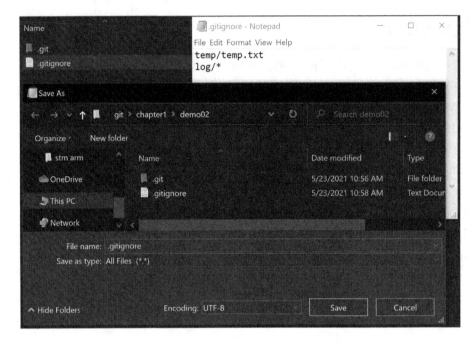

Figure 1-7. *.gitignore includes a list of files and directories to be ignored*

To activate the ignore list, we add the file into the stage area and commit it into the local repository:

```
$ git add .
$ git commit -m ".gitignore added"
```

After committing, suppose `temp.txt` inside the "temp" directory; `Log 1.txt`, `Log 2.txt`, and `Log 3.txt` inside the log folder; and `File1.txt` inside the root of the workspace are created. So the repository has the following organization:

```
ls -R
.:
File1.txt
log/
```

```
temp/
```
./log:
```
Log 1.txt
Log 2.txt
Log 3.txt
```
./temp:
```
temp.txt
```

At this point, the status of the repository is

```
$ git status
```

```
Untracked files:
  (use "git add <file>..." to include in what will be
  committed)
      File1.txt
```

Only File1.txt is detected and listed as a candidate for entering the stage area. The remaining files are ignored because they are already enlisted in the ignore list.

Git only considers files and directories that are created ***after*** committing a .gitignore file. Adding a path or a file that is already staged would not make any effect. To make this point clear, suppose we add File1.txt into the stage area:

```
$ git add File1.txt
```

Then we open the .gitignore file and include File1.txt inside it (Figure 1-8) and commit the updated .gitignore file into the local repository.

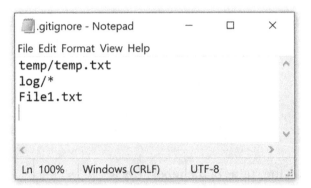

Figure 1-8. *File1.txt is included inside the .gitignore file after we added File1.txt into the stage area*

```
$ git add .gitignore
$ git commit -m "File1.txt added into .gitignore"
```

As File1.txt is included in .gitignore, we expect all changes to the file are ignored. To evaluate this, we add a new line to File1.txt and check the status. If everything were as we expected, then changes on File1.txt would be ignored:

```
Changes not staged for commit:
  (use "git add <file>..." to update what will be committed)
  (use "git restore <file>..." to discard changes in working
  directory)
        modified:   File1.txt
```

Although File1.txt is included in the .gitignore list, the changes are still tracked. For situations like this, to enforce Git to consider the newer version of .gitignore, we need to remove the disinterested files from the stage area, like

```
$ git rm --cache File1.txt
```

The remove command (rm) with the --cache parameter deletes a file from the stage area. If the workspace content does not match with the stage area, we need to use the -f (force) parameter to remove a file forcefully:

```
$ git rm -f --cache File1.txt
```

Ignoring unnecessary files and directories reduces the amount of space consumption and increases access time. For this reason, a template of gitignore is available for different types of projects at https://github.com/github/gitignore.

Inside a Repository

A repository is the magic box of Git. To use Git efficiently, we need to understand the internal of this box. However, there are many concepts and details that hinder enjoyment from the Git ecosystem for typical users. In the following, the essential concepts are introduced and developed through the course of the following chapters.

In the previous sections, we have discussed commits. In a simple but not accurate word, we can imagine a commit is a bag of contents (files and directories) that the user wants to store into the local repository. For each commit Git generates and assigns a unique Id using the contents of the commit, user message, etc. This Id is unique and immutable. So, when a content inside a commit or its message label is changed, Git automatically regenerates a new commit and throws away the old one. Generally, commits are immutable, which means that commits are not allowed to be modified after they are created. When a change happens to a commit, a new one is created from scratch.

Internally, commits are chained together such that each commit is succeeded by the commit that is submitted after it. This chain is called a **branch**. Each commit on a branch can have multiple parents and/or children (Figure 1-9). Normally, the children or parents of a node belong to different branches.

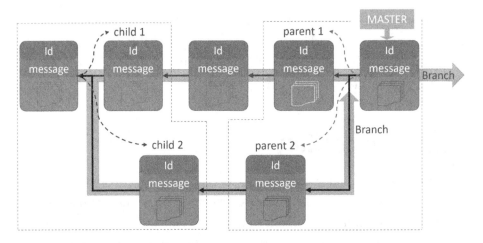

Figure 1-9. *Each commit inside the repository has a unique Id, human-readable label, and one or more parents and children*

Git uses pointers to manage the organization of the branches and commits. We can use these pointers to access a specific point in the history of commits. There are two types of pointers: The first type are automatic pointers. These pointers are constructed automatically by Git and used for managing branches. The most useful pointers in this category are *branch pointers* and *HEAD* pointers. By receiving the very first commit, Git creates the default branch, named *MASTER (in newer trends, it is also called MAIN)*, and inserts the commit into it. The tip commit on the branch is flagged by a branch pointer with the same name as the branch (e.g., MASTER). Branch pointers always point to the last commit on a branch, so when a new commit is inserted into a branch, the branch pointer is automatically updated to point to the new commit. Besides the default branch, we can create other branches, but at each point in time, we are allowed to position on only one of the branches. Git uses a HEAD pointer to mark the current active branch. In contrast to the branch pointers, which are fixed on the last commit, we can reposition HEAD to any commit on any branch. The second type of pointers are labels. We can create labels for commits of interest such that instead of using their Ids, we can use labels to access them. We will discuss labels in the next chapter.

To access a commit, we can use absolute or relative addressing. In absolute addressing we can switch on a commit using its Id. In relative access, the commit position relative to an already known pointer is used. The relative access is very common, and a special syntax is developed for it.

Example

The tilde operator "~" indicates a commit relative to the specific point on the same branch. The left side of the operator is the target pointer, and the right side is the number of commits before the target point:

MASTER~1: One commit before MASTER

MASTER~3: Three commits before MASTER

And generally

Pointer~n: n commit before **Pointer**

In these examples, instead of MASTER, the other pointers could be used. We can also use the absolute address of a commit, for example, 6ca0867~2 means two commits before the commit with Id 6ca0867.

Example

Commits could have multiple parents. This happens when two or more branches are merged. We can specify the parent we need by using the caret operator "^".

> **MASTER^1**: First parent of the commit that
> MASTER points

> **MASTER^2**: Second parent of the commit that
> MASTER points

And in general

> ***Pointer^n***: nth parent of ***Pointer***

Example

The double dot "." is a range operator. It returns the commits in between the selected range.

> **MASTER~4..MASTER~1**: Selects commits in between
> four commits ahead of MASTER (not including the
> fourth one) and the one before MASTER

To make these notations crystal clear, an example application is shown in Figure 1-10. The tilde operator (~) traces the commits on a branch longevity, and the caret operator (^) swifts over branches vertically. For example, the relative address of the second commit of the second parent before MASTER is MASTER^2~2.

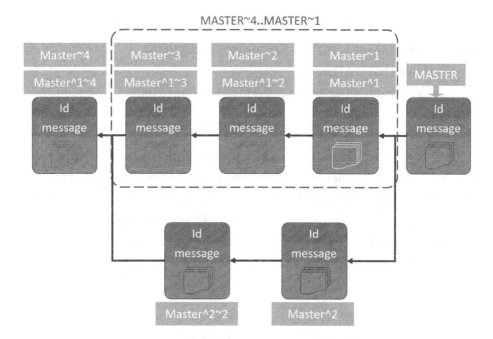

Figure 1-10. *Git supports three types of relative access: the depth operator "~", the horizontal parent operator "^", and the range operator ".." We can access the same note with different addressing patterns: MASTER~2 is the same as MASTER ^1~2*

Log History

The history of commits is kept in the local repository inside the hidden .git directory. Git provides a variety of methods for summarizing and reporting on this history. In this section we will review the log command with the most useful parameters:

```
$ git log

commit 70dda45d728d6fa17e2d7d62629a4cf4f7232b35 (HEAD -> master)
        Author: Altay
        Date:   Thu Aug 12 16:11:39 2021 +0300
```

File2.txt updated

```
commit 19f728d0fd6f0752bb8564c2bc2ba5ed9bd30839
          Author: Altay
          Date:    Thu Aug 12 16:11:15 2021 +0300
```

File1.txt updated

The log command displays complete information for each commit such as author, date and time, Id, and the short text. We can scroll among commits with the up (↑) and down (↓) arrows, and "q" ends the command and returns to the command prompt. The log command provides more concise reports with the oneline parameter. Its output has two columns. The first column is the commit's Id, and the second column is its short message:

```
$ git log --oneline
70dda45 (HEAD -> master) File2.txt updated
19f728d File1.txt updated
80616e8 File3.txt created
e746047 File2.txt created
426242f File1.txt created
```

The stat parameter of the log command reports a summary of changes that happened to files:

```
$ git log --oneline --stat
afe02d1 (HEAD -> master) File1.txt updated
 File1.txt | 3 ++-
 1 file changed, 2 insertions(+), 1 deletion(-)
70dda45 File2.txt updated
 File2.txt | 1 +
 1 file changed, 1 insertion(+)
```

In this example, at the commit with Id afe02d1, File1.txt is changed. With regard to the previous copy of File1.txt, in this commit, three changes, two insertions and one deletion, have happened.

The repository may have dozens of branches, which are interconnected in a complex interconnected network. The graph parameter helps to visualize these interconnections (Figure 1-11):

```
$ git log --oneline --graph
```

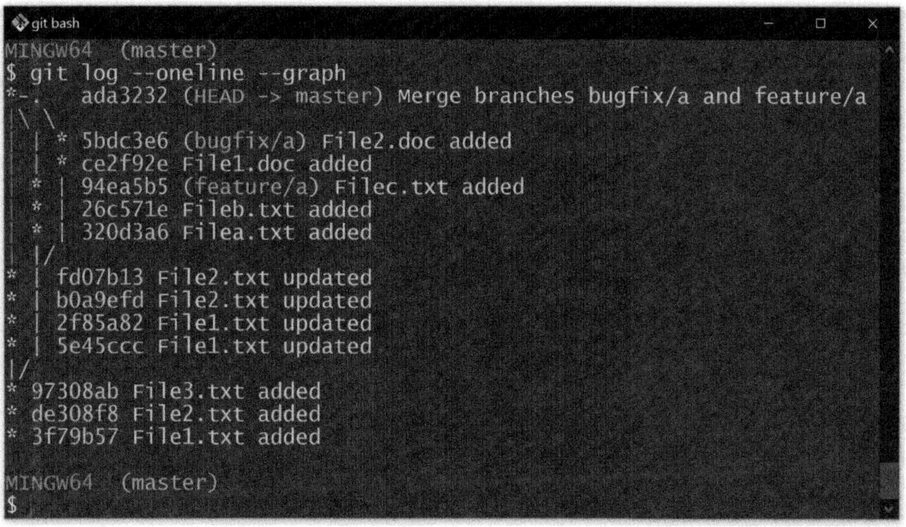

Figure 1-11. The graph parameter provides a visual presentation of the branches

The default order of the log representation is from the latest to the earliest one. The reverse parameter changes this in the other way around:

```
$ git log --oneline
afe02d1 (HEAD -> master) File1.txt updated
70dda45 File2.txt updated
19f728d File1.txt updated
```

```
80616e8 File3.txt created
e746047 File2.txt created
426242f File1.txt created

$ git log --oneline --reverse
426242f File1.txt created
e746047 File2.txt created
80616e8 File3.txt created
19f728d File1.txt updated
70dda45 File2.txt updated
afe02d1 (HEAD -> master) File1.txt updated
```

We can limit the number of reported commits using the range operator (..) or select the latest commits using the -n parameter:

```
$ git log --oneline MASTER~3..MASTER~1
70dda45 File2.txt updated
19f728d File1.txt updated

$ git log --oneline -n 3
afe02d1 (HEAD -> master) File1.txt updated
70dda45 File2.txt updated
19f728d File1.txt updated
```

The range operator picks out commits within the identified boundaries. The number after -n limits the results to commits at the end of the active branch.

To refine the log results based on time and date, we can use the *before, until, since,* and *after* parameters. These parameters accept human-readable strings such as *"yesterday"*, *"last day"*, *"two weeks ago"*, and *"one month ago"* as valid values:

```
$ git log --oneline --before="05-28-2021"
$ git log --oneline --until="one month ago"
```

The `--author` keyword filters the result to commits that are submitted by a specific author:

```
$ git log --oneline --author="Altay"
afe02d1 (HEAD -> master) File1.txt updated
70dda45 File2.txt updated
19f728d File1.txt updated
80616e8 File3.txt created
e746047 File2.txt created
426242f File1.txt created
```

We may require the list of all commits that are directly related to specific issues with no regard to their commit order or time. For example, we may need a list of all commits that are directly related to File1.txt. For these queries, the `--grep` parameter is useful. The grep parameter searches for commits that have the specified string in their message. To have a meaningful result, all commits must have relevant messages; otherwise, grep could not catch them:

```
$ git log --oneline --grep="File1.txt"
afe02d1 (HEAD -> master) File1.txt updated
19f728d File1.txt updated
426242f File1.txt created
```

The grep parameter does not search inside the commits. To find commits where a specific change happened inside them, the `-S""` is used. This parameter, in combination with the `patch` parameter, shows the places where the enquired string is changed. For example, the following command

```
$ git log --patch -S"Line1"
```

searches for all commits in which "Line1" is changed. This change includes all places where Line1 is added to or removed from a file. A sample output is like this:

```
commit 19f728d0fd6f0752bb8564c2bc2ba5ed9bd30839
Author: Altay
Date:    Thu Aug 12 16:11:15 2021 +0300

    File1.txt updated

@@ -0,0 +1,2 @@
+Line1
+Line2
```

We will discuss this result in more detail after we introduce the diff command. At this point it is enough to know that the "Line1" is added to File1.txt in commit 19f728d.

Peek into an Entity

All commits, files and directories *inside* the commits, and all files inside the stage area have their unique identifiers. These Ids are useful when we need to directly access a resource. Indeed, we can think of an Id as a handle that opens the door to a resource (Figure 1-12). The exception of this rule is the physical files in the workspace. Git does not tamper with the source files, so it does not add any Id or metadata to the source files inside the workspace.

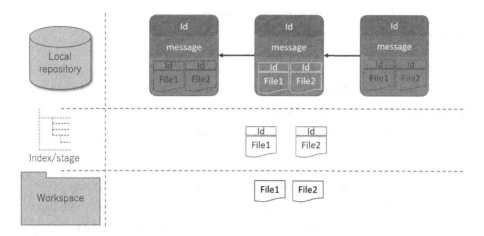

Figure 1-12. *Each resource in each place has a unique Id. We can access them through the Id values*

In the previous section, we saw how the log command returns the commit Ids. In the following, we would extend this knowledge to files inside commits and the stage area. We will figure out methods to see the Ids of the files inside commits and the stage area and then open the file to see the contents of the file.

Inside the Local Repository and Stage Area

The log command lists the commits and their corresponding Ids available inside the repository:

```
$ git log --oneline
630568b (HEAD -> master) File1 and File3 updated
4e9d822 File2.txt updated
761b68d All files updated
31e7044 File4 and File2 updated
5eeb226 File4 added in foo directory
d493c22 Root files updated
80f3e23 Root files created
```

33

The ls-tree command shows the contents of a commit. For example, let's open the 4e9d822 commit:

```
$ git ls-tree 4e9d822
100644 blob 8d29b8d0c4fff2d2fa8732311ef917504cf9c295    File1.txt
100644 blob e944dfcd61d04c4216cc48fb5c32ed53b20570ad    File2.txt
100644 blob 3c4db46784a2eec50021b5d28f28806c7d88d095    File3.txt
040000 tree d7a6244187dfd99d4a661b70321cd3e33df761db    foo
```

In this list, files are marked by "blob" and directories are presented as "tree". Using the show command and the Id, we can open a file or see the contents of the directory. For example, let's see the inside of File1.txt:

```
$ git show 8d29b8d0
Line1
Line2
Line3
Line4
```

Let's see the contents of the foo directory:

```
$ git ls-tree d7a6244
100644 blob
de3bb3fe647d16cffae435b76eb7fcb8e2ae23af    File4.txt
```

File4.txt is inside the foo directory. We can also use relative addressing to access a specific file inside a commit. For example, to see the contents of File1.txt at two commits before the last one on the master branch, we can use

```
$ git show MASTER~2:File1.txt
```

We may need to make sure if a file in the stage area is the same as that in the workspace. In this situation, we use the ls-files command with the stage parameter:

```
$ git ls-file --stage
100644 69acde5d2cd5d3b3397036f739db565d17f63644 0          File1.txt
100644 e944dfcd61d04c4216cc48fb5c32ed53b20570ad 0          File2.txt
100644 8031861ea5001d9873213d8438e9659fface6c06 0          File3.txt
100644 3c4db46784a2eec50021b5d28f28806c7d88d095 0          foo/
                                                            File4.txt
```

We can use the show command to open a file from the stage area:

```
$ git show 3c4db467
Line1
Line2
Line3
Line4
Line5
```

Comparing

Git supports four comparing algorithms – *Myers, Patience, Minimal*, and *Histogram* – to calculate differences between files. These algorithms support comparing files, commits, and branches. The algorithms' steps are different, and sometimes there would be minute differences in their outputs. In the following, instead of discussing technical details of the algorithms, two questions are answered: First, how does comparison work? Then, how is it used? All the examples are based on Myers' algorithm, which is the default comparing method.

How Does Git Compare?

Suppose File1.txt is changed in two different commits as shown in Table 1-1.

35

Table 1-1. *Two versions of File1.txt are stored in two different commits*

Old Version	New Version

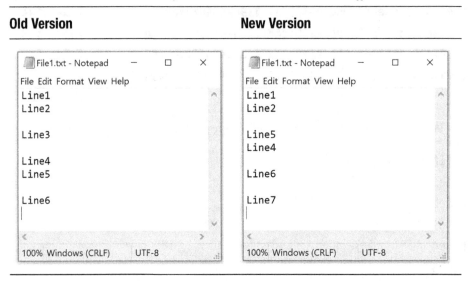

As shown in Table 1-2, Git divides text into subsections. These are (unofficially) called chunks. Each chunk is separated by a blank line.

Table 1-2. *Git splits the texts into separate patches*

Old Version	New Version

Then Git starts analyzing the chunks:

- {Line1,Line2} from the old version reappear in the new version.

- {Line3} exists in the old version, but it is not available in the new version, so this chunk is deleted.

- {Line4,Line5} are inside the old version, but they are changed.

- {Line6} exists in both versions.

- {Line7} is appended to the new version.

Based on these results, the Git output is as shown in Figure 1-13.

Figure 1-13. *Output of comparing two versions of File1.txt*

The plus sign indicates that the corresponding line comes from the new version, the minus sign means that the line was inside the old version and removed from the new version, and white color lines are the same in both versions. For example, Line3 with a minus sign after (which means a blank line) does not exist in the new version. The tricky part of this result is why Line4 is reported two times. To answer this question, let's trace the operations line by line in Figure 1-14.

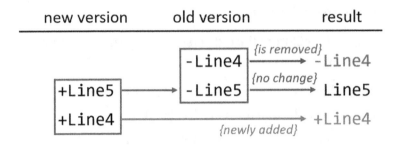

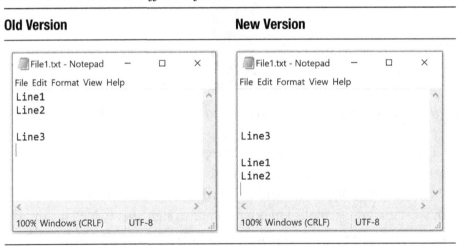

Figure 1-14. *Git compares chunks inside line by line. Line4 from the old content should be removed, and Line4 from the new version should be directly passed to the result*

Example

File1.txt has evolved as shown in Table 1-3. In this example the order of chunks is mirrored with respect to the middle chunk (i.e., Line3).

Table 1-3. *File1 has different forms*

Old Version	New Version

The Git chunks are shown in Table 1-4.

Table 1-4. *Chunks associated with File1.txt*

Old Version	New Version
![File1.txt - Notepad window showing Line1, Line2 boxed together and Line3 boxed separately]	![File1.txt - Notepad window showing an empty box, then Line3 boxed, then Line1, Line2 boxed together]

You noticed that the blank chunk is not escaped. It is considered as an independent chunk and included in comparison operations. As shown in Figure 1-15, the blank chunk in the newer version overwrites the old version contents.

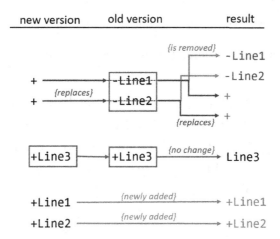

Figure 1-15. *The blank chunk in the newer version overrides the first chunk of the old version*

The Git output is shown in Figure 1-16.

Figure 1-16. *Output of comparing*

The other form of comparison is three-way comparison. In this method three copies of a file are used, and it is often used in merge operations. We will discuss this point in the next chapter.

How to Compare?

With respect to the source and destination, three types of comparison are available:

1. Between the working directory and stage area

2. Between the stage area and local repository

3. Between the working directory and repository

Example

Suppose File1.txt is created, updated, and then committed into the local repository. Again, it is changed and added into the stage area, but before committing, its content in the workspace is changed. So File1.txt has three different forms in each of the workspace, stage area, and local repository (Table 1-5).

Table 1-5. *File1.txt in the workspace, stage area, and local repository*

Workspace	Stage Area	Local Repository
File1.txt - Notepad File Edit Format View Help Line1 Line2 Line3 Line4 < 100% Windows (CRLF)	File1.txt - Notepad File Edit Format View Help Line1 Line2 Line4 Line5 < 100% Windows (CRLF)	File1.txt - Notepad File Edit Format View Help Line1 Line2 Line3 Line4 Line5 < 100% Windows (CRLF)

Let's see the differences between the ***stage area*** and ***workspace***. Example output is shown in Figure 1-17.

```
$ git diff File1.txt
```

Figure 1-17. *Output of the File1.txt comparison between the stage area and workspace*

In this output, --- a/File1.txt is the path to the old copy (in this example, it is in stage area), and +++ b/File1.txt is the path of the new copy, which is in the working directory. In real situations, files may be thousands of lines. To provide concise and effective reports, the diff command does not show whole files, but instead, it detects the differences and then covers them with a few similar lines before and after that location. These sections are headed with @@ @@. The numbers inside the header are a summary: starting from line 1, in total six lines of the old file are included in this report, and starting from line 1, in total seven lines of the new copy are available.

The diff command with the stage parameter compares the last commit in the local repository and the stage area copy. Example output is shown in Figure 1-18.

```
$ git diff --staged -- File1.txt
```

Figure 1-18. *Output of comparing File1.txt in the stage area and local repository*

We can directly compare the content of a commit in the local *repository* with *workspace* content. For example, the following command compares the latest copy of File1.txt in the local repository with the copy available in the workspace (Figure 1-19):

```
$ git diff MASTER -- File1.txt
```

```
--- a/File1.txt
+++ b/File1.txt
@@ -1,6 +1,7 @@
 Line1
+
 Line2
-Line3
+
 Line4
-Line5

+Line5

MINGW64  (master)
$
```

Figure 1-19. *Output of the comparison between the local repository and workspace*

The master is a relative address to the compared commit. It can be changed to any other relative address such as MASTER~n or the Id of a specific commit. A summary of the diff command is shown in Figure 1-20.

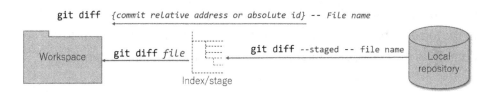

Figure 1-20. *Command flow diagram for comparing a file in different locations*

Using the diff command, we can compare commits. For example, the following command compares f3db6ad and 7451e37:

```
git diff f3db6ad..7451e37 --stat
```

The output is

```
File1.txt | 3 +++
 1 file changed, 3 insertions(+)
```

For a concise report, we can get the names of the files with the name-only parameter, like

```
git diff HEAD~2..HEAD --name-only
```

The output is

```
File1.txt
```

Restore

The add command inserts new contents into the stage area, but is there any way to cancel mistakenly added files from the stage area? Suppose we made some updates on File1.txt inside the workspace, but we noticed the changes were not correct and we needed to return File1.txt to the previous state that it was. For these situations, the restore command is very useful (Figure 1-21).

We can control the domain of restore with its parameters. The default behavior is to restore the workspace and stage area with a copy available in the local repository. However, the stage parameter limits the restore domain to the stage area and does not change the workspace contents.

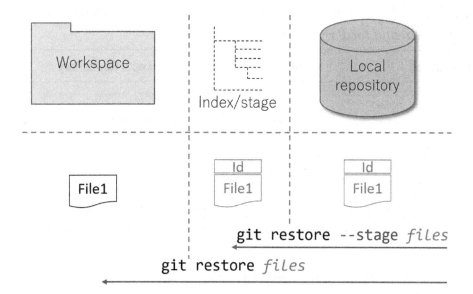

Figure 1-21. *The restore command reverts the files in two levels. With the stage parameter, the files inside the stage area are restored to their previous state, and without the stage parameter, files in both stage and workspace areas are returned to their previous state*

Example

As shown in Table 1-6, File1.txt is stored differently in the workspace, stage area, and local repository.

Table 1-6. *File1.txt has three different contents in the workspace, stage area, and local repository*

Workspace	Stage Area	Local Repository
File1.txt - Notepad File Edit Format View Help Line1 Line2 Line3 Ln 100% Windows (CRLF)	File1.txt - Notepad File Edit Format View Help Line1 Line2 Ln 100% Windows (CRLF)	File1.txt - Notepad File Edit Format View Help Line1 Ln 100% Windows (CRLF)

Let's restore File1.txt in the stage area:

```
$ git restore --stage File1.txt
```

We check the contents of the stage area to see the results. First, we need to acquire the File1.txt Id in the stage area. Then using the show command, we can see its contents:

```
$ git ls-files --stage
100644 98a55606ee136b5d353abeb251a5a341033a4c9b 0
       File1.txt

$ git show 98a55606e
Line1
```

Example

Now we drop the stage parameter and repeat the same example:

```
$ git restore File1.txt
$ git show 98a55606ee1

Line1
```

Let's see the contents of File1.txt in the workspace:

```
cat File1.txt
Line1
```

cat is a Linux command that displays the content of a file. File1.txt inside the stage area and workspace is the same as that in the local repository.

Example

The file temp.txt is not available in the local repository. It is added into the stage area for the first time, but it is not committed yet. The restore command could remove it from this area. Before executing the restore command, we check the status:

```
$ git status
Changes to be committed:
  (use "git restore --staged <file>..." to unstage)
        new file:    temp.txt
```

temp.txt is in the stage area but not committed yet.

```
$ git restore --stage temp.txt
```

After restoring, the status is

```
$ git status
Untracked files:
  (use "git add <file>..." to include in what will be
committed)
        temp.txt
```

For the files that are newly added into the stage area, the restore command with the stage parameter removes them from the stage area; however, it does not erase them from the workspace. So they are categorized as untracked files.

The restore command is not restricted to the latest commit. Using the source parameter, one can determine which specific commit they should restore from:

```
$ git restore --source {commit id} {files name}
```

for example, let's restore File1.txt from commit bf13566:

```
$ git restore --source bf13566 File1.txt
```

Let's restore all contents of the workspace:

```
$ git restore .
```

Reset

The reset command cancels the changes inside a commit. It works in three different levels: inside the local repository only, inside the local repository and stage area, or in all levels (local repository, stage area, and workspace). Respectively, there are three resetting options:

- Soft

- Mixed

- Hard

The command flow graph of these parameters is shown in Figure 1-22. The soft reset relocates the branch pointer to a selected commit, but the stage area and working directory contents do not change. The mixed reset relocates the branch pointer and reloads the stage area with the contents of the selected commit. Finally, the hard reset reloads the stage area and workspace with the contents of the target commit.

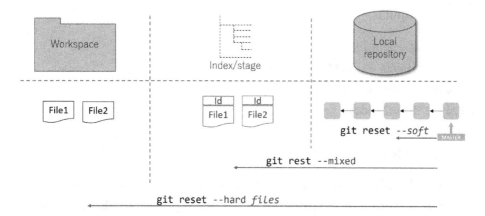

Figure 1-22. *The soft reset relocates the branch pointer, the mixed reset relocates the branch pointer and updates the stage area, and the hard reset updates all levels*

Example

Suppose after creating File1.txt we have five consecutive commits. In each commit a new line is added to the file:

```
$ git log --oneline
0ce0439 (HEAD -> master) Line5 added
a56c5e6 Line4 added
b33459b Line3 added
a974972 Line2 added
be08b6a Line1 added
5290175 File1.txt created
```

A soft reset to MASTER~1 returns the active branch pointer one commit back:

```
$ git reset --soft MASTER~1
```

The output is

```
$ git log --oneline
a56c5e6 (HEAD -> master) Line4 added
b33459b Line3 added
a974972 Line2 added
be08b6a Line1 added
5290175 File1.txt created
```

The relocation of the pointer makes the last commit inaccessible, and the branch keeps growing from the new head. Suppose we add a Line6 to File1.txt:

```
echo Line6>>File1.txt
```

```
Line1
Line2
Line3
Line4
Line5
Line6
```

We add this change to the stage area and commit the changes into the local repository:

```
git commit -am "Line6 added to File1.txt"
[master e3b2d04] Line6 added to File1.txt
 1 file changed, 1 insertion(+)
```

Let's check the log history:

```
$ git log --oneline
e3b2d04 (HEAD -> master) Line6 added to File1.txt
a56c5e6 Line4 added
b33459b Line3 added
```

```
a974972 Line2 added
be08b6a Line1 added
5290175 File1.txt created
```

The previous head commit (0ce0439) is not shown in the log history. This is because the new commit takes its place. You may ask what happened to the 0ce0439 commit. It is inside the local repository for a while. After a period Git will notice this commit has no access, so it removes it from the local repository. We will discuss this point in more detail after introducing Git settings.

Example

The mixed reset updates both the local repository and stage area. To see it in action, we continue with the previous repository. Suppose an empty File2.txt is created, and Line6 is added into File1.txt. These changes are then committed into the local repository:

```
$ git log --oneline
c109ac6 (HEAD -> master) File2 added and File1 updated
0ce0439 Line5 added
a56c5e6 Line4 added
b33459b Line3 added
a974972 Line2 added
be08b6a Line1 added
5290175 File1.txt created
```

Now we reset the repository to one commit before with the mixed parameter:

```
$ git reset --mixed MASTER~1
Unstaged changes after reset:
M       File1.txt
```

To see the effect of the reset command on the local repository, we check the history:

```
$ git log --oneline
0ce0439 (HEAD -> master) Line5 added
a56c5e6 Line4 added
b33459b Line3 added
a974972 Line2 added
be08b6a Line1 added
5290175 File1.txt created
```

The MASTER pointer moved one step back. To see how the stage area is updated, we use the `ls-files` command with the `stage` parameter:

```
$ git ls-files --stage
100644 3c4db46784a2eec50021b5d28f28806c7d88d095 0
        File1.txt
```

To see `File1.txt` in the stage area, the show command is used:

```
$ git show 3c4db46
Line1
Line2
Line3
Line4
Line5
```

You should notice `File2.txt` is removed from the stage area and Line6 is removed from `File1.txt` inside the stage area. These changes are exactly opposite of the last commit. One should notice that these changes did not apply on the workspace contents. So the status is not stable yet, and Git reports some discrepancies exist between the stage area and workspace:

```
$ git status
Changes not staged for commit:
  (use "git add <file>..." to update what will be committed)
  (use "git restore <file>..." to discard changes in working
  directory)
        modified:    File1.txt

Untracked files:
  (use "git add <file>..." to include in what will be committed)
        File2.txt
```

Example

The hard reset returns everything inside the local repository, stage area, and working directory to the selected history point. In continuation of the previous example, we want to return File1.txt to the point at which Line3 is added. First, the commit Id is found using the log command. Then we do a hard reset to the target commit:

```
$ git reset --hard c28455e
HEAD is now at b33459b Line3 added
```

Let's see how the local repository is updated:

```
$ git log --oneline
b33459b (HEAD -> master) Line3 added
a974972 Line2 added
be08b6a Line1 added
5290175 File1.txt created
```

Using the Linux cat command, we can see inside of File1.txt in the workspace:

```
cat File1.txt
Line1
Line2
Line3
```

Revert Without Conflict

The reset command manipulates the history line, and it is totally fine for local repositories. In projects with multiple teams and members who share their commit history, however, it is not safe to tamper with the log history (sometimes it could end up in a complete catastrophe). The revert command undoes changes stored in selected commits while minimizing the risk of history chaos.

The principle of the revert operation is shown in Figure 1-23. In this graph, we want to revert the commit just before the last one (i.e., symbolically indicated by a red circle). The revert command reads inside of that commit and *tries* to revert them back. For this, it considers the commits before and after the target one and then makes a new commit out of them. This new commit is then appended to the end of the branch, and the branch pointer is moved forward. In other words, the revert command deletes a commit by creating another commit, which is exactly in opposition to the target one. This method of removing a point in the log history is very safe for sharing between team members, because nothing is deleted and they only see a new commit is added into the repository.

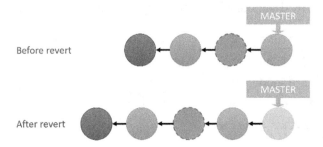

Figure 1-23. *The red commit needs to be canceled. The revert command generates a new commit out of the neighboring commits and appends it to the end of the branch*

Note   The neighboring commits may conflict with each other. So constructing a new commit out of them is not straightforward in all cases. In this section, we focus on not conflicting situations. We will discuss conflicting commit reversion after introducing conflict resolution strategies in the next chapter.

Example

Three commits are submitted into the local repository as shown in Table 1-7. In the first commit, only File1.txt exists. In the second commit, File2.txt is added, but File1.txt is not changed. In the last commit, File1.txt is updated, but nothing changed in File2.txt.

Table 1-7. *Inside HEAD~2 only File1.txt exists; within HEAD~1 File2. txt is created; and inside HEAD only File1.txt is updated*

HEAD~2	HEAD~1	HEAD
File1.txt - Notepad File Edit Format View Help Line1 Line2 Line3 Line4 100% Windows (CRLF)	File1.txt - Notepad File Edit Format View Help Line1 Line2 Line3 Line4 100% Windows (CRLF)	File1.txt - Notepad File Edit Format View Help Line1 Line2 updated Line4 Line5 100% Windows (CRLF)
	File2.txt - Notepad File Edit Format View Help 100% Windows (CRLF)	File2.txt - Notepad File Edit Format View Help 100% Windows (CRLF)

Let's revert a commit before the HEAD:

```
$ git revert HEAD~1
```

As there was no conflict in the neighboring commits, this command opens the default text editor and asks a message for the reverted commit (Figure 1-24).

```
Revert "File2.txt created"

This reverts commit 6d00074864ca6ca05b47d1307f3254f1d41b0953.

# Please enter the commit message for your changes. Lines starting
# with '#' will be ignored, and an empty message aborts the commit.
#
# On branch master
# Changes to be committed:
#       deleted:    File2.txt
```

Figure 1-24. *The revert command automatically opens the default editor for making a new commit message*

The output of the revert command is

```
Removing File2.txt
[master 4c60968] Revert "File2.txt created"
 1 file changed, 0 insertions(+), 0 deletions(-)
 delete mode 100644 File2.txt
```

Using the log command, we can check that the new commit is appended to the branch:

```
$ git log --oneline
4c60968 (HEAD -> master) Revert "File2.txt created"
836b01d File1.txt updated
6d00074 File2.txt created
5ccd82f File1.txt created
```

The revert command removed `File2.txt` from both the workspace and stage area

```
ls
File1.txt

$ git ls-files --stage
100644 e28e390005962e56baa24d466dbfe34c923d945b 0
       File1.txt
```

but it did not remove the reverted commit. So `File2.txt` does exist inside the log history. This is the revert promise. It wraps around the past to cancel its effect. Additionally, the revert command does not change the commit's Id. This feature is critical for keeping the local repository consistent overtime. To see this, we can use the ls-tree command:

```
$ git ls-tree HEAD~2
100644 blob e28e390005962e56baa24d466dbfe34c923d945b    File1.txt
100644 blob e69de29bb2d1d6434b8b29ae775ad8c2e48c5391    File2.txt
```

Get Files Out of a Commit

Using the checkout command, we can extract a set of files from a commit and restore the stage area and workspace contents (Figure 1-25).

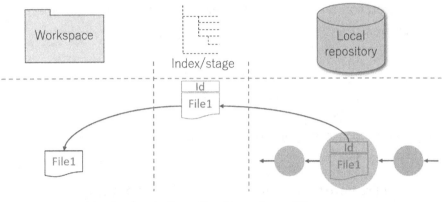

git checkout *{commit address}* -- *files*

Figure 1-25. *The checkout command with file names extracts the target files from the selected commit and updates both stage and workspace contents*

Example

Suppose after creating File1.txt in each commit we add a new line to it. The log history is like

```
$ git log --oneline
eb791a5 (HEAD -> master) Line5 added into File1
10a8df5 Line4 added into File1
5a73d2e Line3 added into File1
fee2b4c Line2 added into File1
a8f300c Line1 added into File1
1ff129f File1.txt created
```

Now we check out File1.txt from three commits before the last one (fee2b4c) and update the workspace and stage area using the extracted commit:

```
$ git checkout HEAD~3 -- File1.txt
```

From now on the File1.txt content in the workspace is

```
cat File1.txt
Line1
Line2
```

Clean Untracked Files

The files removed from the stage area (git rm --cached) are untracked by Git, but they still exist in the workspace. The git clean command is a housekeeping tool that provides a facility to erase untracked files inside the workspace. With the -i parameter, the interactive cleaning menu shows up, and the user can select which files to remove from the workspace.

Example

Suppose File2.txt is inside the workspace but it is not tracked:

```
$ git status
```

```
Untracked files:
  (use "git add <file>..." to include in what will be
  committed)
        File2.txt
```

Let's clean the untracked files:

```
$ git clean -i
```

It opens the command's menu (Figure 1-26). From the items we select 4 to manually control which items should be deleted from the workspace.

```
$ git clean -i
would remove the following item:
  File2.txt
*** Commands ***
    1: clean                 2: filter by pattern    3: select by numbers
    4: ask each              5: quit                 6: help
What now> 4
Remove File2.txt [y/N]? y
Removing File2.txt

MINGW64  (master)
$
```

Figure 1-26. *The clean command with the interactive parameter provides a facility to interactively clean untracked files from the workspace*

To remove untracked directories, the -f (force) and -d (directory) parameters are needed:

```
git clean -fd {directory name}
```

Note   The git clean command may fail due to lack of access permission. In these situations, the command should be executed with super user access permission: sudo git clean -fd.

Summary

In this chapter we have studied the fundamental Git commands. These commands provide the basic operations for interacting with Git:

```
git init {repository name}
git status {--short}
git add {File name}
git commit -m {title message}
git ls-files {--stage}
git show {id}
```

```
git rm {--cache} {-rf} {file name}
git mv {source} {destination}
git log {--oneline} {--graph} {--stat} {-n} {--before =""}
{--until=""} {--author =""}
git ls-tree {commit id}
git diff {--stage} {-- {File name}}
git restore {--stage} {File name}
git reset {--soft/--mixed/--hard} {commit address}
git revert {commit address}
git checkout {commit address} -- {File name}
git clean -i
```

CHAPTER 2

Branches

Branches are like veins within a Git repository. They organize and conceptually give meaning to commits. In this chapter we'll take a comprehensive and applied tour over the most fundamental concepts and commands used for branch operations. We start with the methods to create branches, use them, and manage them and then control the complexity of the local repository.

Overview

During the development of a project, it may require to temporarily divert from the planned milestones. For example, a bug is found, and it requires immediate intervention, or an emergent feature is requested from customers. In these situations, the team leader assigns sub-teams to get in action, while the core developers continue with their scheduled timelines on the master branch. These reactive teams start to work on their own branches; in this way they will not intervene with the work of the core developers. When sub-teams finish their tasks, they merge their branches with the master branch such that all contributions from core developers and sub-teams are unified.

Git branches are pointers. When a new branch is created, nothing is recreated or copied into a new location. All commits remain in their place, and a new pointer is added on the commit chain (Figure 2-1).

© Altay Brusan and Aytac Durmaz 2022
A. Brusan and A. Durmaz, *Git for Electronic Circuit Design*, Maker Innovations Series,
https://doi.org/10.1007/978-1-4842-8124-6_2

Example

There are four commits on the MASTER chain. We create a new branch named FEATURE/A on the last commit.

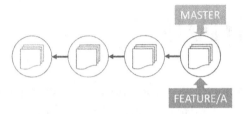

Figure 2-1. *Creating a branch makes a new pointer. FEATURE/A is a new branch made on the last commit*

From this point on, we have two paths to continue: keep adding new commits on the MASTER branch, or switch to the FEATURE/A branch and add commits on it. Adding new commits on the MASTER or FEATURE/A branch makes their corresponding branch pointer move forward (Figure 2-2).

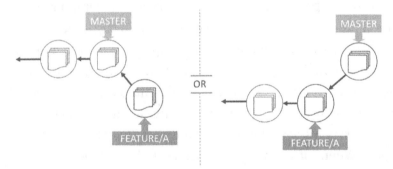

Figure 2-2. *Inserting a commit on a branch moves the branch pointer forward*

Each time only one branch could be active. This is the branch that is marked on the prompt line (Figure 2-3).

Figure 2-3. *The current active branch name (master) is shown on the screen*

How does Git know on which branch it is currently working? For this, Git uses another pointer named HEAD to mark the current active branch. When we switch between branches, HEAD is automatically switched in the background (Figure 2-4). Normally HEAD points to the last commit on the current active branch; however, it is not mandated to be on the last commit all the time. We can move the HEAD position to any commit on the current active branch. This is useful when we need to return the contents of the workspace back to a specific point in time.

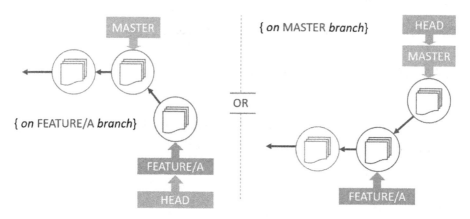

Figure 2-4. *HEAD is always on the active branch*

Creating Branches

We can use the branch command to create a new one:

```
$ git branch FEATURE/A
```

The default form of the command creates a new branch on the commit that HEAD is pointing at. The branch name is not case sensitive. So "FEATURE/A" and "feature/a" are the same. The common naming convention is this: on branches that a new feature is created, the branch name starts with feature (or feat) followed by a slash (/) and then the feature name; on branches that a bug is resolved, the branch name starts with "bugfix/" followed by the bug name (or its code). This is the convention we apply in this book.

To create a branch on another commit, its Id should be used after the branch name, for example:

```
$ git branch FEATURE/A b849b0f
$ git log --oneline

6853984 (HEAD -> master) File2.txt updated
1d4b0fc File1.txt updated
b849b0f (FEATURE/A) File2.txt created
7b669b7 File1.txt created
```

The command creates FEATURE/A on commit b849b0f. Let's see the list of branches:

```
$ git branch

  FEATURE/A
* master
```

The asterisk sign in front of master indicates that master is the current active branch. The other way to find out the active branch is using the status command:

```
$ git status

On branch master
nothing to commit, working tree clean
```

Change the Active Branch

Git has two commands that could be used to change the current active branch. The first option is using the checkout command followed by the target branch name. For example, to switch to the FEATURE/A branch, we can use

```
$ git checkout feature/a
```

If the branch does not already exist, we can use the -b parameter to create the branch. In addition to checkout, we can use the switch command:

```
$ git switch master
```

Creating a branch and switching over to it is a very common practice. For this reason, there is a shortcut in Git. The switch command with the -C (capital C) parameter creates the branch and moves on to this new branch:

```
$ git switch -C FEATURE/B
```

Committed files are local to their branch. By switching between branches, the contents of the working directory change! For example, suppose on branch FEATURE/A File3.txt is created, staged, and committed:

```
MINGW64  (feature/a)
$ ls
File1.txt  File2.txt  File3.txt
```

After switching to the master branch

```
MINGW64   (master)
$ ls
File1.txt   File2.txt
```

we can see that `File3.txt` is not available. It is created, staged, and committed on the FEATURE/A branch.

By switching into another branch, not committed files are transferred to the target branch. For example, suppose File4.txt is created on the master branch and staged but not committed. We switch to FEATURE/A and then check the status:

```
MINGW64   (master)
$ git add File4.txt
```

```
MINGW64   (master)
$ git switch feature/a
Switched to branch 'feature/a'
```
A   *File4.txt*

```
MINGW64   (feature/a)
$ git status
On branch feature/a
Changes to be committed:
  (use "git restore --staged <file>..." to unstage)
        new file:   File4.txt
```

The "A" in front of File4.txt indicates that this file is added to the feature/a stage area. Now, if we commit File4.txt on this branch, it would be local to this branch, and master would not see it anymore:

```
MINGW64   (feature/a)
$ git commit -m "File4.txt is added"
[feature/a 06ec21a] File4.txt is added
```

```
1 file changed, 0 insertions(+), 0 deletions(-)
create mode 100644 File4.txt

$ git switch master
Switched to branch 'master'

MINGW64  (master)
$ ls
File1.txt  File2.txt
```

There are situations where Git does not let switching between branches. This happens when a file has evolved differently on different branches and switching between them requires overriding.

Example

Suppose File1.txt was created on the MASTER branch. At a point in the log history, the feat/a branch is created.[1] File1.txt is updated on both MASTER and feat/a branches independent of each other (Figure 2-5).

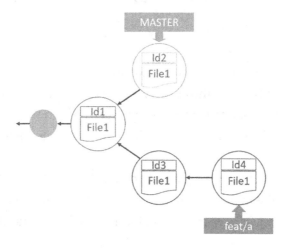

Figure 2-5. *File1 evolved differently on separate branches. This distance makes them incompatible with each other*

---

[1] In software projects, feat is an abbreviation of feature. So feat/a is a short form of feature A, in which A stands for the feature name.

```
$ git log --oneline --all --graph
* 1cdcc28 (HEAD -> master) File1.txt updated
* ed08858 File1.txt updated
| * f179383 (feat/a) File1.txt updated
| * 86fd66c File1.txt updated
|/
* 1791ebb File1.txt updated
* a81ddb9 File1.txt created
```

On the master branch we make some changes on File1.txt and then try to switch over to the feat/a branch without committing the changes:

```
$ git switch feat/a
error: Your local changes to the following files would be
overwritten by checkout:
        File1.txt
Please commit your changes or stash them before you switch
branches.
Aborting
```

This attempt failed because File1.txt already exists on the feat/a branch and it is incompatible with the copy available on the master branch. To solve this issue, we need to commit all changes before switching into another branch or use stash, which is discussed in the following.

Example

Suppose File1.txt is consistent between master and feat/a branches (Figure 2-6). On the master branch, we delete the file, but before committing the change, we try to switch on to the feat/a branch.

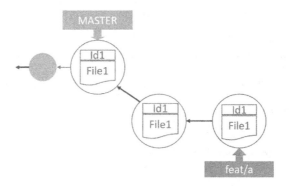

Figure 2-6. *Commits on the feat/a branch do not change File1.txt*

```
$ git log --oneline --graph --all
* 72f11e1 (HEAD -> feat/a) File2.txt updated
* 9883fed File2.txt created
* 78d10c6 (master) File1.txt updated
* b6f3da5 File1.txt updated
* 2355865 File1.txt created

MINGW64  (master)
$ git rm -f File1.txt
rm 'File1.txt'
$ git switch feat/a
Switched to branch 'feat/a'
D       File1.txt
```

The letter "D" in front of File1.txt indicates that File1.txt is deleted. This delete command is transferred to the feat/a branch. If we commit this change on feat/a, then File1.txt will be removed from the feat/a branch; however, it still exists on the master branch. In other words, the changes are stored on the branch that they are committed on, not the branch that starts the changes.

```
$ git commit -am "File1.txt deleted"
[feat/a 40d66d4] File1.txt deleted
 1 file changed, 4 deletions(-)
 delete mode 100644 File1.txt

MINGW64  (feat/a)
$ git switch master
Switched to branch 'master'

MINGW64  (master)
$ ls
File1.txt
```

Change the Branch Name

The branch command with the -m parameter changes the branch's name. The first name is the old name, and the second one is the branch's new name:

```
git branch -m feat/a feat/b

$ git branch
  feat/b
* master
```

Delete a Branch

Let's delete an empty branch:

```
$ git branch -d feat/a
$ git log --oneline --all --graph
* 575e766 (HEAD -> master) File1.txt updated
* 3c856e4 File1.txt updated
```

```
* b66b813 (feat/a) File1.txt updated
* 7a62e33 File1.txt created

MINGW64  (master)
$ git branch -d feat/a
Deleted branch feat/a (was b66b813).

MINGW64  (master)
$ git log --oneline --all --graph
* 575e766 (HEAD -> master) File1.txt updated
* 3c856e4 File1.txt updated
* b66b813 File1.txt updated
* 7a62e33 File1.txt created
```

Note   It is not possible to delete an active branch. If we need to delete a branch that we are working on, we first switch to another branch and then delete it.

The feat/a branch is empty before the branch is deleted. After deleting the branch, the feat/a pointer is removed; however, the commit the pointer was pointing at is still available.

To delete a non-empty branch, it is required to merge it; otherwise, the commits on that branch would be lost. Nonetheless, if we were sure that the commits are not required anymore, then we could enforce Git to remove an unmerged branch as well all commits on it:

```
git branch -D feat/b

$ git log --oneline --graph --all
* ca0f091 (HEAD -> master) File1.txt updated
| * 3fcdbce (feat/b) File2.txt updated
| * 8a47c0c File2.txt updated
```

```
| * 835d1dc File2.txt created
|/
* 47c087f File1.txt created

MINGW64  (master)
$ git branch -D feat/b
Deleted branch feat/b (was 3fcdbce).

MINGW64  (master)
$ git log --oneline --graph --all
* ca0f091 (HEAD -> master) File1.txt updated
* 47c087f File1.txt created
```

The capital "D" enforces the deletion operation.

Compare Branches

The log command with the {*source branch*}..{*destination branch*} parameter lists all commits that are available on {destination branch} but not included on {source branch}:

```
git log --oneline {source}..{destination}
```

```
$ git log --oneline --graph --all
* 6f00275 (HEAD -> master) File3.txt created
* 3ca0fc9 Files updated
| * e830828 (feat/a) File2.txt updated
| * 6d9f52b File1.txt updated
|/
* f673374 File2.txt updated
* 70aa1b4 File1.txt updated
* c15f034 File1.txt created
```

```
$ git log --oneline master..feat/a
e830828 (feat/a) File2.txt updated
6d9f52b File1.txt updated
```

```
$ git log --oneline feat/a..master
6f00275 (HEAD -> master) File3.txt created
3ca0fc9 Files updated
```

The master..feat/a parameter shows commits on feat/a but not on master. The feat/b..master parameter shows commits only on master.

We know that the most updated version of files is available in the last commit of the branches. So, to compare between two branches, we need to differentiate the tips of the branches. The diff command implements this functionality (Figure 2-7).

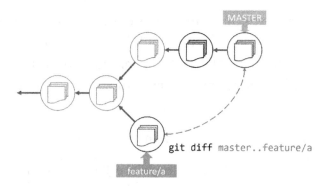

Figure 2-7. *The diff command compares the tips of branches*

```
git diff feat/b..master
--- a/File2.txt
+++ b/File2.txt
@@ -1,4 +1,4 @@
 Line1
-Line0
 Line2
 Line3
+Line4
```

Like comparing commits, we can use other parameters such as --stat and --filename to refine the diff results.

Stash

Git avoids switching between branches if it involves overwriting a file. One solution is to commit the changes before switching. Commits are bricks of history, and there should be a meaningful reason to have them inside the local repository – switching between branches seems to be far from a logical reason to have a commit. For this situation, Git has a temporary storage that stores the changes inside and lets us freely move between branches without need to make a new commit.

Example

Suppose File1.txt evolved differently on feat/a and MASTER branches such that they are not compatible with each other. We make a change on File1.txt on the MASTER branch, and before committing it, we try to switch to feat/a, which is not possible. We insert File1.txt into stash:

```
$ git stash push -m "File1 in stash"
```

```
Saved working directory and index state On master: File1
inserted in stash
```

This command encapsulates working directory and stage area contents and then inserts them into the stash area with the given message. Stash is a zero-index stack, and multiple entries could be inserted into it. To see the results, we can use the status command:

```
$ git status
On branch master
nothing to commit, working tree clean
```

Let's see the list of the items in stash:

```
$ git stash list
stash@{0}: On master: File1 inserted in stash
```

We have inserted an entity into stash. It is the first item, and its index is zero. To restore the content of an entity, we can use the apply command followed by the stash index we need to reload:

```
$ git stash apply 0

On branch master
Changes not staged for commit:
  (use "git add <file>..." to update what will be committed)
  (use "git restore <file>..." to discard changes in working
  directory)
        modified:    File1.txt
```

This command reloads the first entry contents (index zero) onto the working directory.

Note   Stash accepts staged files only. So, if you add a new file that is not already entered into the stage area, then stash will not encapsulate it. In this situation you need to use the -m parameter to include all staged and not staged files.

Let's delete a stash entry (one by one):

```
git stash drop 0
Dropped refs/stash@{0}
(5c4b613aaf379997097166c96212e77182cd3bd9)
```

Or we can remove all entries at once:

```
git stash clear
```

77

Move on a Branch

The HEAD pointer normally points to the last commit on the active branch. However, we can manually relocate the position of the HEAD pointer. This relocation is useful for temporarily checking the content of a specific commit:

```
git log --oneline
c172859 (HEAD -> master) File1.txt updated
2b8f56f File1.txt updated
adc3cd4 File1.txt updated
7b43f9d File1.txt created

MINGW64  (master)
$ git checkout adc3cd4
Note: switching to 'adc3cd4'.

You are in 'detached HEAD' state. You can look around, make
experimental
changes and commit them, and you can discard any commits you
make in this
state without impacting any branches by switching back to
a branch.
...
HEAD is now at adc3cd4 File1.txt updated

MINGW64  ((adc3cd4...))
$
```

The command takes HEAD to the adc3cd4 commit. Git warns that HEAD is detached from the branch. In this mode, we can read files but are not allowed to make any updates or changes. The reason is that Git commits are immutable, so when they are stored in the local repository, they are closed from further intervention. If we try to make a change in the contents of a commit, Git creates a new commit. However, in a detached situation, HEAD is temporarily relocated. So, after returning it to the tip of the branch, the newly created commit would be inaccessible (Figure 2-8).

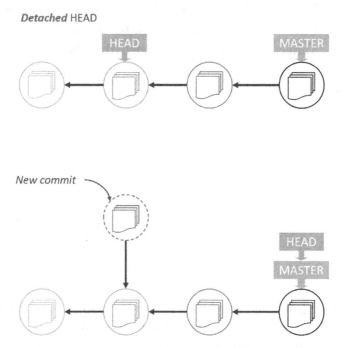

Figure 2-8. *Changes made in detached mode are stored in a new commit. After returning HEAD to the branch's tip point, the new commit is not accessible*

To exit the detached state, we can use the checkout command with the branch name. For example, on the master branch to exit the detached situation, we can use

$ git checkout master

Merge Branches

Branches grow up independent of each other, and sometimes later they merge to reunify their contents (Figure 2-9). At the merge point, some files may conflict with each other. To resolve this issue, Git has a special tool named *mergetool*, which helps to decide on the conflicting points. Git supports a variety of merging algorithms. In the following, the most common merging algorithms and conflicting situations and the way that Git resolves conflicts are discussed.

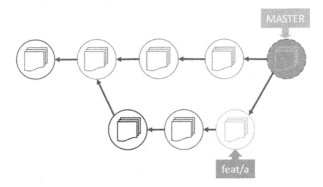

Figure 2-9. *Branches are independent of each other. At the merge point, they come together to reunify the history lines. At this point conflict can occur that should be resolved*

Fast-Forward Merge

The fast-forward (FF) merge is the simplest form of merging two branches. This merge happens when the branches are linearly accessible and one branch is just a few commits ahead from the other one (Figure 2-10).

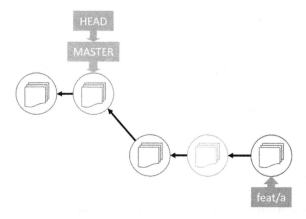

Figure 2-10. *Fast-forward merge happens in situations in which one branch is ahead of another one and they are linearly accessible*

Suppose "master" and "feat/a" branches are needed to be merged. The log history before merge is like this:

```
$ git log --oneline --all
f93c0ee (feat/a) File1.txt updated
737e799 File1.txt updated
667da1b (HEAD -> master) File1.txt updated
7b4cd9f File1.txt updated
6b877c2 File1.txt updated
fd4c0df File1.txt created
```

On the master branch, we can order to merge it with feat/a using the merge command:

```
git merge feat/a
Updating 667da1b..f93c0ee
Fast-forward
 File1.txt | 4 ++--
 1 file changed, 2 insertions(+), 2 deletions(-)
```

The output of the merge is

```
git log --oneline --all
f93c0ee (HEAD -> master, feat/a) File1.txt updated
737e799 File1.txt updated
667da1b File1.txt updated
7b4cd9f File1.txt updated
6b877c2 File1.txt updated
fd4c0df File1.txt created
```

The master branch is moved forward and points to "feat/a".
Simultaneously, the HEAD pointer also shifts to master's position
(Figure 2-11).

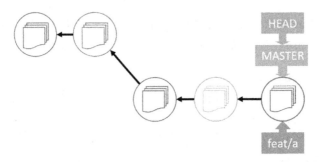

Figure 2-11. *After fast-forward merge, two branches point to the*
same commit

After merge, there is no need for the old branch, and it could be
deleted:

```
git branch -d feat/a
```

In fast-forward merging, the master pointer moves forward, and no
new merge commit is created. Sometimes it is good to know at which point
two branches are merged into each other. To enforce this requirement, we
can use the no fast-forward, `--no-ff`, option:

```
git merge --no-ff feat/a
Merge made by the 'recursive' strategy.
 File1.txt | 4 ++--
 1 file changed, 2 insertions(+), 2 deletions(-)
```

It automatically opens the default text editor and asks the user for the merge point's commit message (Figure 2-12).

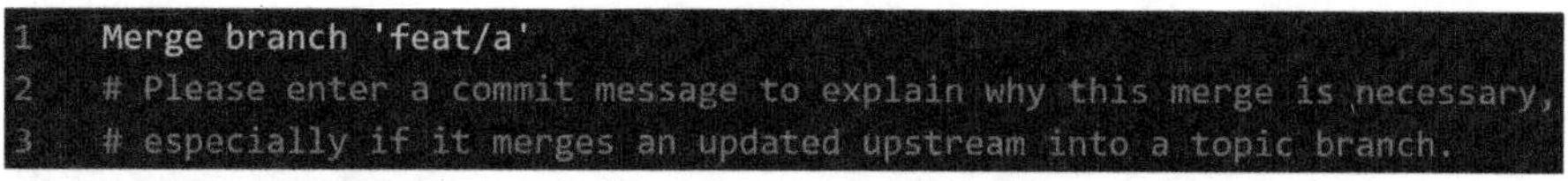

```
1    Merge branch 'feat/a'
2    # Please enter a commit message to explain why this merge is necessary,
3    # especially if it merges an updated upstream into a topic branch.
```

Figure 2-12. *With the no fast-forward option, the default text editor opens and asks the user for the new commit merge message*

We can check that a new commit is created:

```
MINGW64  (master)
$ git log --oneline --all --graph
*   2480f8c (HEAD -> master) Merge branch 'feat/a'
|\
| * f93c0ee (feat/a) File1.txt updated
| * 737e799 File1.txt updated
|/
* 667da1b File1.txt updated
* 7b4cd9f File1.txt updated
* 6b877c2 File1.txt updated
* fd4c0df File1.txt created
```

Three-Way Merge

The three-way merge is the most common but tricky merge type. In this merge, files are updated on two branches, and later the branches reunify at the merge point (Figure 2-13). For this, Git analyzes each chunk (you can imagine chunks as sections that are separated by a blank line) of the base file separately using the following rules:

- If a chunk does not change on a branch, it is directly copied from base to the target.

- If a change on a chunk happens on only one branch, that change is considered as the new version of the chunk, and it is used at the merge point.

- If both branches make a change on the same chunk, then a conflict happens, and the user is needed to decide.

- If a chunk is added on both branches but it is not available on the common base, then it is added into the merge point.

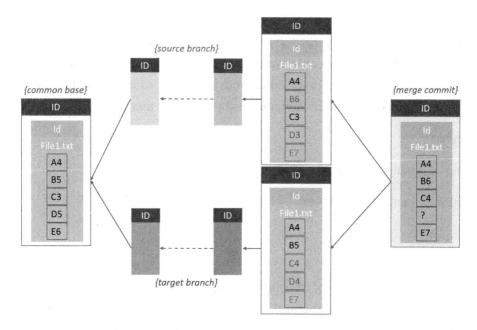

Figure 2-13. *Three-way merge: A file passes through two different branches and evolves differently at each branch. To merge branches, Git uses the last commits on each branch and the common base of both commits to compare the files*

Example

File1.txt is prepared based on the contents shown in Table 2-1.

Table 2-1. *File1.txt contents in the common base, master branch, and feat/a branch*

Common Base	Master Branch	Feat/a Branch
Chunk1	Chunk1	Chunk1
Chunk2	Chunk2	Chunk2 changed on feat/a
Chunk3	Chunk3 changed on master	Chunk3
	Chunk4	Chunk4

Chunk1 is not changed on both branches, so it appears as is. Chunk2 and Chunk3 are updated on one branch. Based on the merge rule, the most updated version is copied to the output. Chunk4 does not exist on the common base, but it is added on both branches, so it is copied to the output. Based on the three-way merge, the resulting merge commit is

Chunk1

Chunk2 changed on feat/a

Chunk3 changed on master

Chunk4

Example

In this example one of the branches appends a chunk to File1.txt, and the other changes another chunk. Contents of File1.txt are available in Table 2-2.

Table 2-2. *File1.txt contents in the common base and master and feat/a branch tip points*

Common Base	Master Branch	Feat/a Branch
Chunk1	Chunk1 changed on master	Chunk1
Chunk2	Chunk2	Chunk2
		Chunk3

On the master branch Chunk1 is changed, and on the feat/a branch Chunk3 is appended. The output of the merge is

Chunk1 changed on master

Chunk2

Chunk3

Example

Suppose a chunk is added in between two other chunks in File1.txt. Complete contents of File1.txt on each branch are available in Table 2-3.

Table 2-3. *File1.txt contents in the common base, master branch, and feat/a*

Common Base	Master Branch	Feat/a Branch
Chunk1	Chunk1 changed on master	Chunk1
Chunk2	Chunk middle on master	Chunk2
	Chunk2	Chunk3

The output of the merge is

Chunk1 changed on master

Chunk middle on master

Chunk2

Chunk3

Example

As shown in Table 2-4, on one branch more than one chunk is added such that the *number of chunks* is not equal.

Table 2-4. *File1.txt contents in the common base and master and feat/a branches*

Common Base	Master Branch	Feat/a Branch
Chunk1	Chunk1 changed on master	Chunk1
Chunk2	Chunk2	Chunk2
	Chunk3	Chunk3
	Chunk4	
	Chunk5	

The output of the merge is

```
Auto-merging File1.txt
CONFLICT (content): Merge conflict in File1.txt
Automatic merge failed; fix conflicts and then commit
the result.
```

Git complains about a conflict. It happened at the end of the file. Chunk4 and Chunk5 are available on the master branch but do not exist on feat/a. We need to decide which branch should dominate the result. Should Chunk4 and Chunk5 from master be copied to the output or "nothing" from feat/a? We will discuss how to resolve the conflicts in the following.

Example

Suppose in the common base Chunk1 and Chunk2 are available in File1.txt. These chunks do not change on feat/a, but on the master branch, Chunk2 is deleted (Table 2-5).

Table 2-5. *File1.txt contents in the common base and master branch and "feat/a" branches*

Common Base	Master Branch	Feat/a Branch
Chunk1	Chunk1	Chunk1
Chunk2		Chunk2

The output of this merge is

Chunk1

Any changes on one branch takes precedence over the previous data. In this example, this change was deleting Chunk2 on the master branch, and it overwrites the unchanged branch content.

Example

A summary of the contents of File1.txt is available in Table 2-6. We try to merge master and "feat/a" branches.

Table 2-6. *File1.txt on master and "feat/a" branches. On the master branch Chunk4 and Chunk5 and on the feat/a branch Chunk1 and Chunk3 are replaced by a blank space*

Common Base	Master Branch	Feat/a Branch
Chunk1	Chunk1	Chunk2
Chunk2	Chunk2	Chunk4
Chunk3	Chunk3	Chunk5
Chunk4		
Chunk5		

On the master branch Chunk4 and Chunk5 are erased but not deleted. In other words, Chunk4 and Chunk5 are replaced by blank lines. On the feat/a branch Chunk1 and Chunk3 are replaced by an empty line. Git considers these empty lines as the corresponding deleted chunks and eliminates them. The output of the merge is

Chunk2

As we see no conflicts happened. Let's repeat the same example but completely remove chunks without inserting blank lines (Table 2-7).

Table 2-7. *File1.txt in the common base and on master and feat/a branches*

Common Base	Master Branch	Feat/a Branch
Chunk1	Chunk1	Chunk2
Chunk2	Chunk2	Chunk4
Chunk3	Chunk3	Chunk5
Chunk4		
Chunk5		

Git warns that conflicts have happened:

```
Auto-merging File1.txt
CONFLICT (content): Merge conflict in File1.txt
Automatic merge failed; fix conflicts and then commit
the result.
```

This is because in Git's eye File1.txt at the common base has five chunks, on the tip of the master branch it has three chunks, and on the feat/a branch it has different chunks. When we try to merge them, the number of chunks does not match, and Git warns about conflicts.

The rules we have discussed are not limited to chunks inside files. They are also applicable to files inside the workspace. For example, new files created on a branch are also copied to the merge commit, and files that are deleted on one branch are removed from the merge commit.

Example

The common base commit has three files, File1.txt, File2.txt, and File3.txt. On the feat/a branch File2.txt is removed. On the master branch File3.txt is removed, File4.txt is added, and some changes are made on File1.txt (Table 2-8).

Table 2-8. *Workspace content in the common base and master branch and feat/a branch tip points before merge*

Common Base	Master Branch	Feat/a Branch
File1.txt	File1.txt (updated)	File1.txt
File2.txt	File2.txt	File3.txt
File3.txt	File4.txt	

After merge, the contents of the workspace are

```
File1.txt (updated)
File4.txt
```

Merge Flowchart

Conflict happens when each branch changes a chunk differently. In this case Git points out the list of conflicting files, and we need to go through all the conflicting files and resolve the conflicts inside one by one. Identifying conflict points and resolving them is a time-consuming and complex process. To ease the process, there are tools that help with merging such as *KDiff*, *P4merge*, *WinMerge*, and *Visual Studio*. In the following we use Visual Studio Code as the default merge tool.

How to Configure Microsoft Visual Studio Code as the Default Merging Tool

1. Install Visual Studio Code.
2. Run the following commands:
   - `git config --global merge.tool vscode`
   - `git config --global diff.tool vscode`
3. Run
   - `git config --global -e`
4. Append the following lines to the .gitconfig file:

```
[mergetool "vscode"]
    cmd = "code --wait $MERGED"
[diff]
    tool = vscode
[difftool "vscode"]
    cmd = "code --wait --diff  $LOCAL $REMOTE"
```

5. Save changes and close Visual Studio Code.

Conflict prevents the compilation of a merge. When a conflict happens, Git enters a *merging* state (Figure 2-14):

```
$ git merge feat/a
```

```
Auto-merging File1.txt
CONFLICT (content): Merge conflict in File1.txt
Automatic merge failed; fix conflicts and then commit the result.

MINGW64  (master|MERGING)
$
```

Figure 2-14. *Merging state: This state appears when there is a conflict between commits and we need to resolve it*

The prompt changes to (master|MERGING). In this state we should interactively dissolve the conflicts. The conflict resolution flowchart is shown in Figure 2-15. In a merging state, the merge tool provides us three options:

- Abort the merge using the git merge --abort command.

- Call mergetool using the git mergetool command.

- Continue after all conflicts are resolved by git merge --continue.

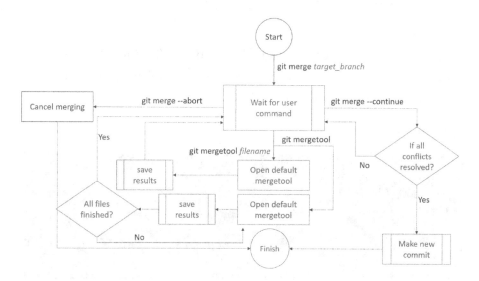

Figure 2-15. *Merge state flowchart*

Calling the mergetool command with a file name opens the merge tool (e.g., Microsoft Visual Studio Code) for resolving conflicts for that file. However, calling the command without any file name automatically opens the merge tool for all conflicting files one after another. When we finish the merge operation, we can continue with the --continue parameter, which leads to making a new commit out of all resolved files.

Example

Due to conflicts between File1.txt copies on master and feat/a branches, the merge command is stopped and enters a merge state:

```
$ git merge feat/a
Auto-merging File1.txt
CONFLICT (content): Merge conflict in File1.txt
Automatic merge failed; fix conflicts and then commit
the result.

MINGW64  (master|MERGING)
$
```

To resolve them we call mergetool without any file name (Figure 2-16). Otherwise, by providing the file name after mergetool, we can specify which file we aim to resolve for conflicts.

```
$ git mergetool
```

Figure 2-16. *Chunk4 comes from the master branch, and a blank space and Chunk2 are incoming changes from the feat/a branch*

The ======= is the separation line. All lines between <<<<<<< HEAD and ======= come from the source branch on which the merge command is invoked (in this case, it is master). All lines between ======= and >>>>>>> feat/a come from the target branch, which in this example is feat/a. At this point there is only one conflicting point. If there were more than one issue, we would need to resolve them too.

To solve a conflict, we have three options:

1. Keep only the source lines.

2. Keep only the destination lines.

3. Keep both branches' lines.

We decide to save the source branch and discard the changes made on the destination. The output is

Chunk1

Chunk3
Chunk4

Chunk2

In Visual Studio Code we need to save the changes and then quit. Git notices the updates and automatically returns to the merging state. If there were another file, then we would need to repeat the same steps for that file too. After finishing with all files, we continue with merging:

```
$ git merge --continue
```

This command opens the default text editor (Figure 2-17). We can enter a message and a description for the new merge commit.

```
Merge branch 'feat/a'

# Conflicts:
#    File1.txt
#
# It looks like you may be committing a merge.
# If this is not correct, please run
#    git update-ref -d MERGE_HEAD
# and try again.
```

Figure 2-17. *Default text editor in which we can enter a message for the new commit*

When we save the changes and close the tool, Git automatically quits from the merging state and appends the new merge commit into the history:

```
$ git log --oneline --graph -all
*   be498f9 (HEAD -> master) Merge branch 'feat/a'
|\
| * 9c49c73 (feat/a) File1.txt updated
* | 92fd380 File1.txt updated
|/
* c76fde5 File1.txt updated
* 4343242 File1.txt created
```

Squash Merge

Making a new branch, fixing some issues on it, and merging it back to the master branch is a common practice. However, by increasing the repetition of this cycle, the repository history is polluted by many small branches with a few commits on them. To avoid the curse of branches and keeping them manageable, Git offers squash merge. As shown in Figure 2-18, in this merge, a new commit is made from commits on another branch and added to the tail of the active branch.

Before squash merge   after squash merge

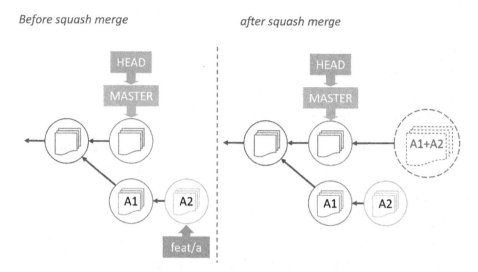

Figure 2-18. *Squash merge combines multiple commits on a feat/a branch and makes a new one. This new commit is added to the tail of the master branch*

Example

On the master branch File1.txt is created and updated in three commits. At one point a feat/a branch is created. On this branch File2.txt is created and updated. Then we return to the master branch and update File1.txt:

```
$ git log --oneline --all --graph
* 9aeb2c9 (HEAD -> master) File1.txt updated
| * a0e023b (feat/a) File2.txt updated
| * fad996e File2.txt updated
|/
* f8c7a10 File1.txt updated
* b74694f File1.txt updated
* 96106db File1.txt updated
```

Now we want to squash feat/a on master:

```
$ git merge --squash feat/a
Automatic merge went well; stopped before committing as
requested
Squash commit -- not updating HEAD
```

There is no conflict, and Git added File2.txt from feat/a to the master branch. We need to commit this file into the local repository:

```
$ git status
On branch master
Changes to be committed:
  (use "git restore --staged <file>..." to unstage)
        new file:   File2.txt
```

To finalize the squash merge, we need to commit it:

```
$ git commit -m "Feat/a branch squashed"
[master 9017d45] Feat/a branch squashed
 1 file changed, 3 insertions(+)
 create mode 100644 File2.txt
```

Example

As shown in Table 2-9, File1.txt is updated on both master and "feat/a" branches. We want to squash feat/a onto master.

Table 2-9. *Contents of File1.txt on master and "feat/a" branches*

Master Branch	Feat/a Branch
Line1	Line1
Line2	Line2
	Line3
Line3	
	Line4
Line5	

There is a conflict between two versions. The output of the squash merge is

```
Auto-merging File1.txt
CONFLICT (content): Merge conflict in File1.txt
Squash commit -- not updating HEAD
Automatic merge failed; fix conflicts and then commit
the result.
```

If we take a look inside File1.txt in the workspace, we would notice Git already added conflict marks into the file (Figure 2-19).

```
Line1
Line2

Line3

<<<<<<< HEAD
Line5

=======
Line4
>>>>>>> feat/a
```

Figure 2-19. *The conflict points are marked by Git. At the end of File1.txt, conflicts are marked by Git before invoking the mergetool*

Using mergetool, we can solve conflicts (Figure 2-20):

```
$ git mergetool File1.txt
```

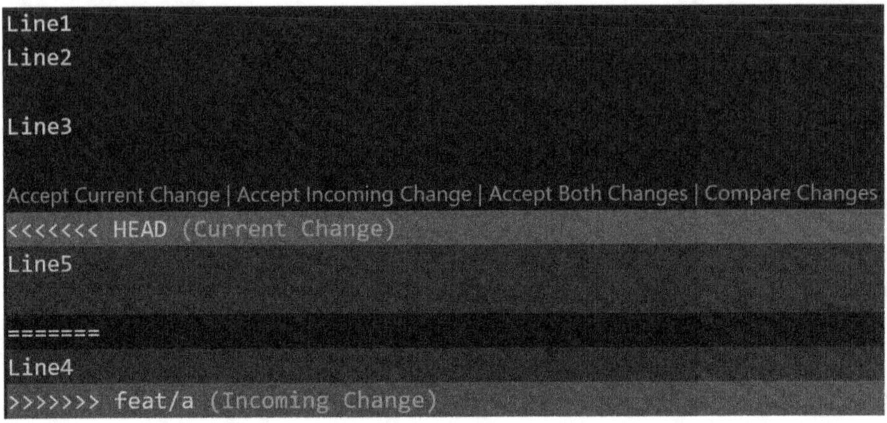

```
Line1
Line2

Line3

Accept Current Change | Accept Incoming Change | Accept Both Changes | Compare Changes
<<<<<<< HEAD (Current Change)
Line5


=======
Line4
>>>>>>> feat/a (Incoming Change)
```

Figure 2-20. *mergetool opens the marked File1.txt and shows the options for resolving the conflicts*

After making our selections, the conflicts are resolved, and changes are saved into the workspace. During squash merge, "orig" files may be created. These files are backup files and automatically generated by Git. After merge, we can safely remove them:

```
rm *.orig
```

To store the squashed commit permanently, we need to commit it:

```
$ git commit -m "File1.txt squash merged"
```

At the end we can delete the branch:

```
$ git branch -D feat/a
```

Rebasing

The rebase command changes the base of a branch to another commit (Figure 2-21).

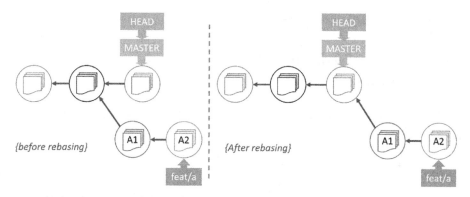

Figure 2-21. *The rebase command changes the base commit of a branch. "Feat/a" is relocated to the end of the master branch*

Normally, rebasing is used for linearly integrating a branch into the local master branch. It helps to keep the log history clean and consistent. As shown in Figure 2-21, after rebasing the master branch is linearly behind the feat/a branch, and a fast-forward merge is needed to move the master branch ahead.

Rebasing should be used in local repositories. The projects that are shared between multiple team members could crash if a member rebases a branch. How might it happen? The rebase command rewrites the history! As we have already mentioned, commits are immutable and cannot be changed after being stored in the local repository. When a branch is rebased, behind the scenes, Git makes copies of the commits on that branch and ties them up to the new place. These replicas have different Ids, so they do not match with the other team members' log history. Sharing the repository with different commit Ids would crash the others' repository.

Example

The feat/a branch includes three commits. Inside these commits File1. txt is updated such that it conflicts with File1.txt on the master branch:

```
$ git log --oneline --all --graph
* 64bfc16 (HEAD -> master) File1.txt updated
| * dd6f8b2 (Feat/a) File1.txt updated
```

```
| * 4b2cef2 File1.txt updated
|/
* 6895e7a File1.txt updated
* 38b2b23 File1.txt created
```

To rebase feat/a onto the master branch, at first, we need to switch on feat/a:

```
$ git switch feat/a
```

We can interactively participate in resolving possible conflicts. For this, we use the rebase command with the -i parameter:

```
$ git rebase -i master
```

This command opens the To-Do dialog. Inside this list we can order a command for each commit on the feat/a branch (Figure 2-22).

```
pick 4b2cef2 File1.txt updated
pick dd6f8b2 File1.txt updated

# Rebase 64bfc16..dd6f8b2 onto 64bfc16 (2 commands)
#
# Commands:
# p, pick <commit> = use commit
# r, reword <commit> = use commit, but edit the commit message
# e, edit <commit> = use commit, but stop for amending
# s, squash <commit> = use commit, but meld into previous commit
# f, fixup <commit> = like "squash", but discard this commit's log message
# x, exec <command> = run command (the rest of the line) using shell
# b, break = stop here (continue rebase later with 'git rebase --continue')
# d, drop <commit> = remove commit
# l, label <label> = label current HEAD with a name
# t, reset <label> = reset HEAD to a label
# m, merge [-C <commit> | -c <commit>] <label> [# <oneline>]
```

Figure 2-22. To-Do list dialog of the interactive rebase command. For each commit, we can select a command to apply on that commit

In front of each commit, there is a placeholder for the command to be applied on that commit. The default command is "pick." We can replace it with an item from the list. We select the edit command for all commits (Figure 2-23).

```
edit 4b2cef2 File1.txt updated
edit dd6f8b2 File1.txt updated
```

Figure 2-23. *For each commit, we select the edit command. This command lets us resolve the potential conflicts*

Then we save the list and close the editor. This automatically returns us to the Bash environment:

```
git rebase -i master
error: could not apply 6a0e4a9... File1.txt updated
Resolve all conflicts manually, mark them as resolved with
"git add/rm <conflicted_files>", then run "git rebase
--continue".
You can instead skip this commit: run "git rebase --skip".
To abort and get back to the state before "git rebase", run
"git rebase --abort".
Could not apply 6a0e4a9... File1.txt updated
Auto-merging File1.txt
CONFLICT (content): Merge conflict in File1.txt

MINGW64  (feat/a|REBASE 1/2)
```

The prompt sign indicates that the state is in the middle of rebasing. There are two commits on the "feat/a" branch, and currently the first commit is under review for rebasing (1/2 means the first commit from a total of two commits). In this commit File1.txt conflicts with the master File1.txt (Figure 2-24). To resolve this, we use mergetool:

```
$ git mergetool File1.txt
```

```
Line2
Accept Current Change | Accept Incoming Change | Accept Both Changes | Compare Changes
<<<<<<< HEAD (Current Change)

Line1


=======
>>>>>>> 4b2cef2 (File1.txt updated) (Incoming Change)
Line3

Line4
```

Figure 2-24. *Conflicts may happen while rebasing a branch. We need to resolve them with mergetool*

We accept both changes, save the document, and close mergetool to return to the Bash environment. To proceed with the next commit, we need to call the continue command:

$ git rebase --continue

Before proceeding with the next commit, Git makes a new commit out of the updates made on the first commit so far and asks for a message for this new commit.

After, Git starts to make a replica for the second commit. This is shown in the command prompt by

MINGW64 (feat/a|REBASE 2/2)

You may notice that File1.txt on the master branch is updated to the merge output made from the first commit on the feat/a branch and the last commit on the master branch. The updated copy of File1.txt is used for evaluating the second commit on feat/a. In other words, to rebase the second commit on "feat/a," the new version of File1.txt is used. After all conflicts are resolved, we have

```
git log --oneline --all --graph
```

```
* 3ce53b9 (feat/a) File1.txt updated
* 4dc20d1 File1.txt updated
* 44c5783 (HEAD -> master) File1.txt updated
* 8e68eb3 File1.txt updated
* 4fc166a File1.txt created
* 0ed69f6 File1.txt created
```

After rebasing feat/a, it is linearly accessible from the master branch. We can do a fast-forward merge to make them synchronized and then delete feat/a.

Example

On the master branch File1.txt, File2.txt, and File3.txt are created and Line1 is added into File1.txt. On this commit the feat/a branch is created. On the master branch File3.txt is updated, while on the feat/a branch File2.txt is removed, File1.txt is changed, and File4.txt is created. The log history is summarized in Table 2-10.

```
* dbad8dc (HEAD -> master) File3.txt updated
| * 9a6dcb4 (feat/a) File4.txt added
| * 4586ffc File1.txt Updated
| * 2b78136 File2.txt deleted
|/
* 07b0b97 File1.txt Updated
* c116058 All files created
```

Table 2-10. *Contents of the workspace on the master and feat/a branches and the place the feat/a is joined to master*

Common Base	Master Branch	Feat/a Branch
File1.txt	File1.txt	File1.txt
File2.txt	File2.txt	(updated)
File3.txt	File3.txt	File3.txt
	File3.txt	File4.txt
	(updated)	

We switch to the feat/a branch and start rebasing it over master:

```
$ git rebase -i master
```

In the To-Do list we select to edit all commits:

```
edit 2b78136 File2.txt deleted
edit 4586ffc File1.txt Updated
edit 9a6dcb4 File4.txt added
```

There is no conflict between the commits on the feat/a branch and master, so we can continue with rebasing for all three commits:

```
$ git rebase -continue
```

After merging master with feat/a, File2.txt is removed, File4.txt is added, and File1.txt is updated. The content of the workspace is

```
File1.txt  File3.txt  File4.txt
```

Cherry-Pick

A commit may be submitted into the wrong branch. To cancel this, we can reset the commit and submit the changes to the correct branch, or we may use the cherry-pick command. This command copies a subset of commits from a branch to another one (Figure 2-25).

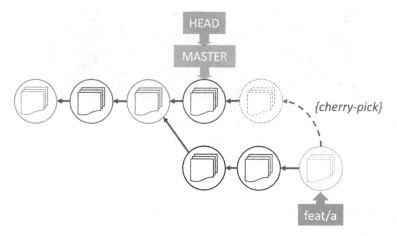

Figure 2-25. *Cherry-pick moves a subset of commits from one branch to another*

Example

The local repository has two branches: feat/a and master. The history of the repository is like the following:

```
* 08ac685 (HEAD -> master) File1.txt updated
| * acf235c (Feat/a) File2.txt created
| * 5fcc065 File1.txt updated
|/
* 4658417 File1.txt updated
* 6ba9629 File1.txt created
```

We need to move the last commit from feat/a to the master branch:

```
$ git cherry-pick -e acf235c
```

The command creates a new commit out of the 185a6b7 commit. The -e parameter edits the new commit's message before recreation (Figure 2-26).

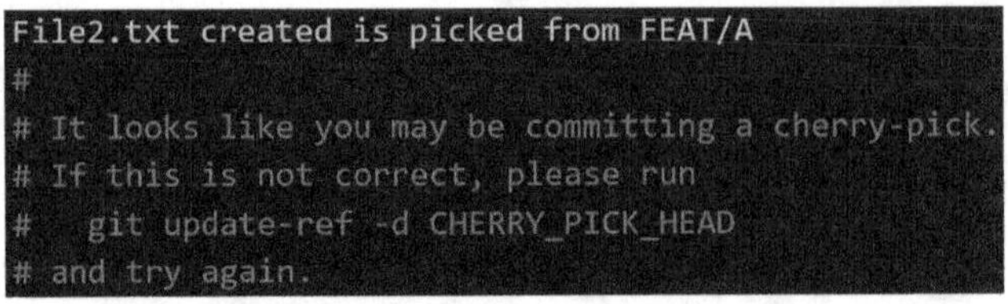

Figure 2-26. *A new commit message dialog automatically appears when the -e parameter is used with cherry-pick*

After submitting the message and closing the editor

```
* 5c3ce5b (HEAD -> master) File2.txt created is picked
from FEAT/A
* 08ac685 File1.txt updated
| * acf235c (Feat/a) File2.txt created
| * 5fcc065 File1.txt updated
|/
* 4658417 File1.txt updated
* 6ba9629 File1.txt created
```

the new commit is added on the master branch. You should notice the picked commit is not removed from the feat/a branch.

Example

In the previous example, we select the commit with Id 5fcc065 and move it onto the master branch:

```
$ git cherry-pick -e 5fcc065
```

In this commit File1.txt is updated, which is inconsistent with File1.txt on the master branch. We need to resolve this in the cherry-picking state:

```
Auto-merging File1.txt
CONFLICT (content): Merge conflict in File1.txt
error: could not apply 5fcc065... File1.txt updated
MINGW64  (master|CHERRY-PICKING)
```

To solve conflicts, we use mergetool:

```
$ git mergetool File1.txt
```

After resolving File1.txt conflicts, we continue with the other conflicting files:

```
$ git cherry-pick –continue
```

After resolving all conflicts in all conflicting files, we submit a commit to store the results:

```
$ git commit -m "File1.txt cherry-pick updated"
```

Cancel a Merge

Merging branches is an error-prone operation. We may make mistakes while resolving conflicts. To retrieve the operation back, we have two options, which are discussed in the following. These commands are more useful if they are applied soon after a wrong merge commit; otherwise, the history line of the logs may collapse.

The first method to cancel a merge commit is to reset the HEAD pointer to the commit before the merge point. In this way, the last commit is deprived, and Git removes it later.

Example

Suppose we have the following log history in our local repository:

```
*   84a328b (HEAD -> master) Merge branch 'feat/a'
|\
| * 86b9380 (feat/a) File.txt updated
| * 5f684ab File.txt updated
* | a2bad9d File.txt updated
|/
* cd67b7c File.txt updated
* 5f2f5a3 File.txt created
```

We can reset the merge commit using the reset command:

```
$ git reset --hard HEAD~1
```

The log history after becomes

```
* a2bad9d (HEAD -> master) File.txt updated
| * 86b9380 (feat/a) File.txt updated
| * 5f684ab File.txt updated
|/
* cd67b7c File.txt updated
* 5f2f5a3 File.txt created
```

The second method to cancel a merge is using the revert command:

```
git revert -m 1 HEAD
```

After merging, HEAD points to the newly created merge commit. The revert command cancels out the effect of this commit. A merge commit has two parents: one is on the source branch, and the other is on the target branch. The parameter -m identifies which parent to revert to. As shown in Figure 2-27, the master branch is parent 1, and the feat/a branch is parent 2.

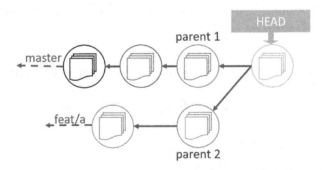

Figure 2-27. *A merge commit has more than one parent. The first parent is on the source branch (e.g., master), and the other is on the target branch (e.g., feat/a)*

The revert command creates a new commit, which cancels the merge commit.

Revert with Conflicts

In simple applications the revert command has no conflict. In real-world scenarios, conflicts happen while reverting a commit. Git resolves the conflicts with a three-way merge algorithm; the reverted node is the common base, and the commits before and after it are the tip points (Figure 2-28).

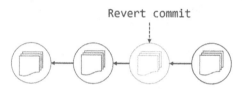

Figure 2-28. *The reverted commit is the common tip point, and the neighboring commits are the other tips used by the three-way merge algorithm to resolve the conflicts*

Example

File1.txt has three different contents in three consecutive commits, and we need to revert the middle one (Table 2-11).

Table 2-11. *Content of File1.txt before, after, and at the reverted commit. The blank lines are empty spaces that discriminate between chunks*

HEAD~2	Reverted Commit	HEAD
Line1	Line1	Line1
Line2	Line2	Line2
Line3	Line8	Line6
Line4		Line7
	Line6	
Line5	Line7	Line2
		Line3
Line6		

Reverting this commit causes conflict:

```
$ git revert HEAD~1
Auto-merging File1.txt
CONFLICT (content): Merge conflict in File1.txt
error: could not revert 8921c79... File1.txt updated
MINGW64  (master|REVERTING)
```

The command enters a reverting state. Like three-way merge, the user has options:

- Resolve the conflicts using mergetool: git mergetool
- Skip the current conflicting commit: git revert --skip
- Continue with the next step: git revert --continue
- Abort the revert operation: git revert --abort

In this example, we accept both changes. The content of File1.txt is

```
Line1
Line2

Line6
Line7

Line2
Line3

Line3
Line4

Line5

Line6
```

The changes are saved, and mergetool is closed, and we proceed with the next steps:

```
$ git revert --continue
```

It automatically opens the default text editor and asks for the new commit message (Figure 2-29).

```
Revert "File1.txt updated"

This reverts commit 8921c79e71f7a5d75310659a924e97189a86f896.
```

Figure 2-29. *revert creates a new commit and asks for a message for the commit*

After the editor is closed, Git automatically creates a new commit with the message that we provided.

Example

A series of commits are reversible using the range operator (..) in one command. To make it simple, suppose each commit adds a new line to File1. txt (Figure 2-30). We need to revert the last three commits behind HEAD.

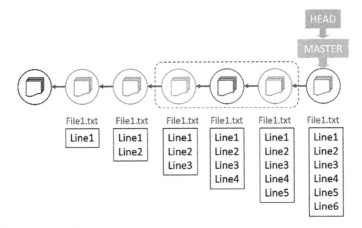

Figure 2-30. *In each commit a new line is added to File1.txt*

For this we use

```
$ git revert HEAD~4..HEAD~1
```

In this command HEAD~4 is used instead of HEAD~3. This is because the last commit (HEAD~4) is not included in the range. The revert command starts to revert all changes from HEAD~1, HEAD~2, and HEAD~3. However, due to conflict, Git enters a reverting state:

```
Auto-merging File1.txt
CONFLICT (content): Merge conflict in File1.txt
error: could not revert 11e478a... File1.txt updated
hint: after resolving the conflicts, mark the corrected paths
hint: with 'git add <paths>' or 'git rm <paths>'
hint: and commit the result with 'git commit'

MINGW64  (master|REVERTING)
```

The first reverting commit that needs to be resolved is HEAD~1. HEAD~2 and HEAD are used to solve the conflict. On HEAD we have six lines, but on HEAD~2 there are four lines. The last two lines exist on only one commit but are not available on the other (Figure 2-31).

```
git mergetool File1.txt
```

```
Line1
Line2
Line3
Line4
Accept Current Change | Accept Incoming Change | Accept Both Changes | Compare Changes
<<<<<<< HEAD (Current Change)
Line5
Line6
=======
>>>>>>> parent of 11e478a (File1.txt updated) (Incoming Change)
```

Figure 2-31. *For the first reverting commit, HEAD~1, the conflict happened between HEAD and HEAD~2*

For this example, we accept the incoming changes and save the changes. To proceed with reverting, we use the `continue` command; however, before proceeding with the next commit, the text editor shows up and asks for a commit message. This message is used for the newly created reverted commit:

```
git revert --continue
```

The process of resolving conflicts and committing the updates is repeated for all commits inside the target range. The final output is

```
c3d1c58 (HEAD -> master) Revert "Line3 inserted into File1.txt"
7744355 Revert "Line4 inserted into File1.txt"
34dce80 Revert "Line5 inserted into File1.txt"
```

Restore

The restore command extracts file(s) from a source:

$ git restore --source {name or id} -- {Full_File_name}

The source is the Id of the commit we want to extract a file from, and the file name is the complete file name that includes path folders in which the file is located.

Example

The following command restores File3.txt from commit 5a57dae:

```
$ git restore --source 5a57dae -- File3.txt
```

We can use the branch name to bring the copy of file(s) from that branch into the current branch:

```
git restore --source feat/a -- File2.txt
```

The restore command copies the target file(s) from source into the workspace. To keep it in the local branch, we need to add the file(s) into the stage area and then commit it (them) into the repository:

```
$ git restore --source feat/a -- File1.txt
$ git status
On branch master
Changes not staged for commit:
  (use "git add <file>..." to update what will be committed)
  (use "git restore <file>..." to discard changes in working
  directory)
        modified:   File1.txt

no changes added to commit (use "git add" and/or "git
commit -a")
```

We can limit the restored file into the stage area with the `--stage` parameter. This parameter updates the file in the stage area:

```
$ git restore --staged --source feat/a -- File1.txt
```

Tag

Tags are marks inserted on commits, and they are useful to quickly access those commits. They are especially useful for marking release commits at the end of a development cycle. Some web services automatically encapsulate all contents of a tagged commit into a single compressed file. Git supports two types of quick and complete tags, which are discussed in the following.

Example

On the master branch, the main course of the project has been developed. After a while, a new feature is added to the project on the feat/a branch. The development of this feature is finished, and the branch is merged to master. This is the place we want to release a version. We can add a tag to the merge point such that in the future we can directly access it:

```
git tag v1.0 a62a34c
*   a62a34c (HEAD -> master) Merge branch 'feat/A'
|\
| * b175ac5 (feat/a) File2.txt updated
| * 6c61ba4 File1.txt updated
| * 16ab6c2 File2.txt created
* | a45dd34 File1.txt updated
* | 365ec18 File1.txt updated
|/
* bc06d8a File1.txt updated
* 4f1db29 File1.txt created
```

We can jump to the place the tag is inserted, using the checkout command:

```
git checkout V1.0
```

Calling the tag command without any parameter lists all tags:

```
$ git tag
v1.0
```

To remove a tag, we can use the delete parameter. This parameter removes the tag and does not erase the commit itself:

```
$ git tag --delete V1.0
Deleted tag 'v1.0' (was a62a34c)
```

To add an annotated tag, we can use the -am parameters (-a is the short form of annotated tag, and -m means message):

```
git tag -am "Release version 1.0" V1.0 HEAD
```

Let's see the list of all annotated and unannotated tags:

```
git tag -n
v1.0                 Release version 1.0
```

Summary

Conflicts are unavoidable while working with a multitude of branches. However, we should have a firm understanding about the reasons for the conflicts and tools that we have for resolving them. In the next chapter, we will use this information in a collaborative environment. A summary of the commands that we used follows:

```
git branch {branch_name}
git branch -m {old_name} {new_name}
git branch -d {branch_to_be_deleted}

git checkout {branch_name/commit_id}

git switch -C {branch_name}

git log --oneline {source_branch}..{dest_branch}
git diff source_branch_name..destination_branch_name

git merge {--no-ff} {--squash} branch_name

git rebase -i {branch_name}
git cherry-pick -e {commit_id}
git revert {target_commit}
git restore {--staged} {--source} branch_name -- File_name
```

CHAPTER 3

Remote Repository

Storing the history of the contributions on local computers is usually useful as a backup mechanism in small and private projects. In real-world applications, the sheer number of contributors and commits requires having a common placeholder to manage the file sharing between contributors. In this regard, the Git repository model is very flexible and dexterous. It supports both centralized and distributed repository architectures for sharing projects between peers (Figure 3-1).

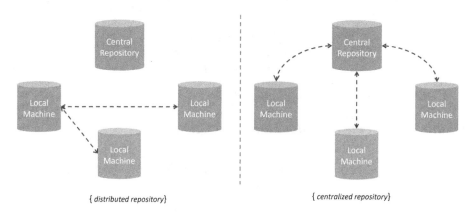

{ distributed repository} { centralized repository}

Figure 3-1. *Git supports both centralized and distributed repository models*

The central repository storage service is provided by third-party companies such as GitHub, Bitbucket, GitLab, etc. The charging policy of the providers is different and could change overtime. In addition to online providers, some organizations, due to security and privacy issues, prefer to

© Altay Brusan and Aytac Durmaz 2022
A. Brusan and A. Durmaz, *Git for Electronic Circuit Design*, Maker Innovations Series,
https://doi.org/10.1007/978-1-4842-8124-6_3

use private Git networks. In the following we will use GitHub as a remote Git repository provider; however, the topics are applicable to the other providers.

The central repository that hosts contributions is called a *remote* repository. The term *remote* does not necessarily mean that the data is collected on the cloud or in a far place. However, it emphasizes that the data is stored in a place other than the local machine – it could be on a machine within a private network.

Create a Repository in GitHub

The first step to create a repository in GitHub is to have an account. After creating an account and successfully signing in, we can create a new repository.

Create your first project

Ready to start building? Create a repository for a new idea or bring over an existing repository to keep contributing to it.

Create repository   Import repository

Figure 3-2. *Create repository dialog in GitHub*

By clicking Create repository, the basic repository creation form shows up.

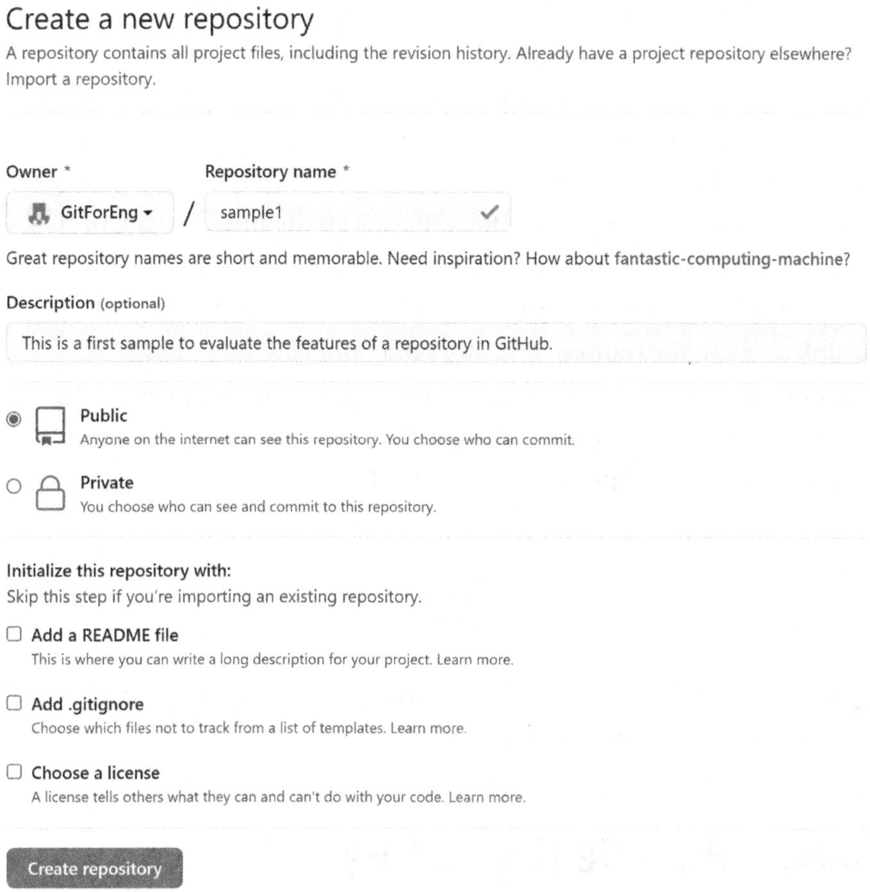

Create a new repository

A repository contains all project files, including the revision history. Already have a project repository elsewhere? Import a repository.

Owner *   Repository name *

🎐 GitForEng ▾   /   sample1   ✓

Great repository names are short and memorable. Need inspiration? How about fantastic-computing-machine?

Description (optional)

This is a first sample to evaluate the features of a repository in GitHub.

◉ 📖 **Public**
        Anyone on the internet can see this repository. You choose who can commit.

○ 🔒 **Private**
        You choose who can see and commit to this repository.

Initialize this repository with:
Skip this step if you're importing an existing repository.

☐ **Add a README file**
      This is where you can write a long description for your project. Learn more.

☐ **Add .gitignore**
      Choose which files not to track from a list of templates. Learn more.

☐ **Choose a license**
      A license tells others what they can and can't do with your code. Learn more.

Create repository

Figure 3-3. *Create a new repository dialog in GitHub. An empty sample1 repository with no readme, ignore, and license files is created*

It is a good practice to assign the project or product name as the repository name. Public repositories are visible to the world, but private ones are just accessible to the invited community. In this demo, we have made the "sample1" repository public so that the readers could see its contents. We can create automatically generated readme, gitignore, and license files by checking their corresponding check boxes; however, the more preferred practice is to add them in separate commits. In this way we can manipulate each file separately. Having a well-documented readme file is very useful for open source projects, because users can learn about the project using the readme contents. Providing a suitable license file (e.g., CC-BY-3.0, gpl, lgpl-2.1, etc.) is very crucial for open source projects: first, it protects the author's legal responsibilities; second, a good license agreement could protect the author's credit and financial profits from their contributions in open source projects.

In GitHub each repository has a unique access link. We can use this link to clone the remote repository or connect to the remote repository to send data into it (Figure 3-4). For normal applications the HTTPS communication protocol is good enough; however, in secure environments the SSH protocol is preferred.

Figure 3-4. *GitHub repository link access. We can access a GitHub repository using either HTTPS or SSH*

Clone a Remote Repository

A remote repository is cloned into a local machine using the clone command. We can specify the remote repository address and an optional folder name in which the remote repository is cloned:

```
$ git clone https://github.com/GitForEng/sample1.git demo01
Cloning into 'demo01'...
warning: You appear to have cloned an empty repository.
```

In this example, the remote repository sample1 is cloned into the demo01 folder. Cloning an empty repository is somehow an exception. There is no branch in the repository, and Git warns about this issue.

Cloning a repository automatically replicates all remote branches on a local machine. Large-scale projects have a considerable number of commits and data branches, which include only bulks of backup data. Cloning the complete project would take a lot of time and disk space. In these scenarios, we can confine the cloning to a specific subset of branches.

Example

Suppose the remote repository has three branches: master, feat/a, and bugfix/a. We are interested in cloning the feat/a branch only. We can use

```
$ git clone --branch feat/a --single-branch https://github.com/
GitForEng/sample1.git demo02
```

The command fetches the "feat/a" branch only and checks it out. Let's see the list of all remote branches:

```
$ git branch --remote
  origin/bugfix/a
```

The remote repository's address is `https://github.com/GitForEng/sample1.git`; however, when the repository is cloned, Git assigns an alias name "origin" to it. This is useful for making stuff more concise and human-readable. So origin/feat/a semantically represents feat/a on origin and always tracks the remote branch. Additionally, Git automatically creates a local branch in the local repository named feat/a, which follows the origin/feat/a branch:

```
$ git branch --all
* feat/a
  remotes/origin/feat/a
```

In this example "feat/a" is a local branch that tracks the remotes/origin/feat/a branch. The "remotes" specifically indicates that the branch origin/feat/a follows a remote repository.

Push, Fetch, Pull Commands

Till now, an empty repository is cloned, and a commit is submitted to its local master branch (Figure 3-5 A). The push command sends the *local active* branch (i.e., master) to the remote repository and then creates a new branch named origin/master to follow up the updates happening in the remote repository master branch. To understand the difference between master and origin/master, suppose a new commit is inserted into the master branch (Figure 3-5 B). HEAD and the local master branch move ahead, but origin/master does not change (Figure 3-5 C). However, after pushing the new commit to the remote repository, the origin/master position is also updated automatically and placed at the commit that HEAD is pointing at (Figure 3-5 D). We need to emphasize that recently GitHub renamed "master" branches into "main."

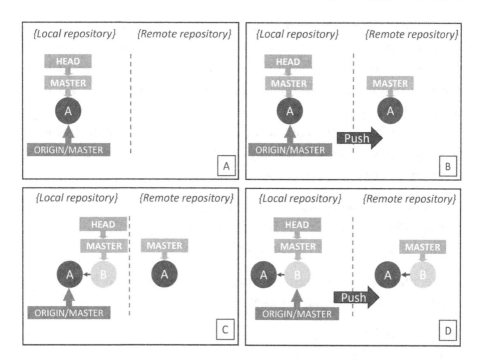

Figure 3-5. *(A) An empty remote repository is cloned, and a commit is added into it. (B) A new commit is inserted in the master branch. (C) This local change updates HEAD and the master branch but does not affect the origin/master branch. The commit is pushed to the remote repository. (D) This sends the new commit to the remote repository and updates the origin/master branch*

The Git push command facilitates us to send the current active branch to the remote repository. The basic form of the push command is

```
$ git push origin
Enumerating objects: 3, done.
Counting objects: 100% (3/3), done.
Writing objects: 100% (3/3), 220 bytes | 220.00 KiB/s, done.
Total 3 (delta 0), reused 0 (delta 0), pack-reused 0
To https://github.com/GitForEng/sample2.git
 * [new branch]      master -> master
```

The command calculates the changes that are required to be transferred from the local repository into the remote repository named *origin*. Git noticed that there was no branch in the local repository that follows the remote master branch. For this reason, it created a new branch and named it `origin/master`.

A new commit is added on the local master. This will update the local master branch but does not have any effect on the remote `origin/master`. We can check this out using the log command:

```
$ git log --oneline --all
004f6a9 (HEAD -> master) file1.txt updated
9e509ac (origin/master) file1.txt created
```

After pushing the commit, `origin/master` is updated too. It will move to the last commit that HEAD points at:

```
$ git push origin
$ git log --oneline --all
004f6a9 (HEAD -> master, origin/master) file1.txt updated
9e509ac file1.txt created
```

The default branch that is pushed is the current active branch (the branch that HEAD is pointed at). However, we can specify the branch name that we are interested in. For example, let's push `feat/a` to `origin`:

```
$ git push origin feat/a
```

```
To https://github.com/GitForEng/sample2.git
 * [new branch]      feat/a -> feat/a
```

The feat/a branch is pushed to the remote repository, and origin/feat/a is created to follow the remote branch.

Let's push all branches at once:

```
git push --all origin
```

To delete a remote branch (not a local one), we can use the delete parameter followed by the branch name. For example, suppose we have three branches feat/a, bugfix/a, and master in our local repository followed by their counterpart branches origin/feat/a, origin/bugfix/a, and origin/master:

```
$ git branch --all
  bugfix/a
  feat/a
* master
  remotes/origin/bugfix/a
  remotes/origin/feat/a
  remotes/origin/master
```

To delete "feat/a" from origin, we use the push command with the following syntax:

```
$ git push --delete origin feat/a
remote: This repository moved. Please use the new location:
remote:    https://github.com/GitForEng/Sample1.git
To https://github.com/GitForEng/sample1.git
 - [deleted]         feat/a
```

We can check the results using the branch command followed by the --all parameter, like

```
$ git branch --all
  bugfix/a
  feat/a
* master
  remotes/origin/bugfix/a
  remotes/origin/master
```

Suppose a team member adds a new commit to the remote repository, which is not available in our local repository (Figure 3-6).

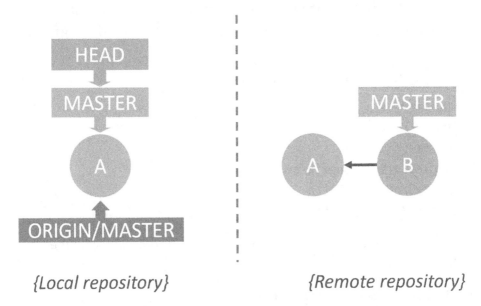

{Local repository}   *{Remote repository}*

Figure 3-6. *A new commit is submitted to the remote repository by another team member. This commit is not yet available in our local repository*

The fetch command loads the new commit from the remote repository into the local repository and updates the origin/master branch (Figure 3-7).

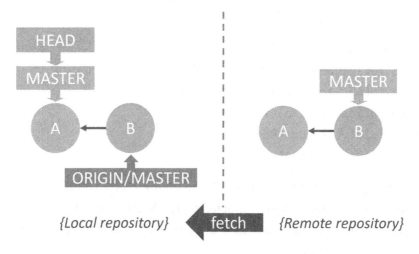

Figure 3-7. *The fetch command loads remote repository branch contents into the local repository tracking branch*

Using the log command, we check the branch points in the local repository:

```
$ git log --oneline
5d4eff4 (HEAD -> master, origin/master, origin/HEAD) file1.
txt updated
004f6a9 file1.txt updated
9e509ac file1.txt created
```

We fetch the remote repository updates into the local repository:

```
$ git fetch origin
remote: Enumerating objects: 5, done.
remote: Counting objects: 100% (5/5), done.
remote: Total 3 (delta 0), reused 3 (delta 0), pack-reused 0
Unpacking objects: 100% (3/3), 246 bytes | 49.00 KiB/s, done.
From https://github.com/GitForEng/sample2
   5d4eff4..452a918  master      -> origin/master
```

Let's see the results of the fetch command:

```
$ git log --oneline --all
452a918 (origin/master, origin/HEAD) file1.txt updated
5d4eff4 (HEAD -> master) file1.txt updated
e4f15c0 (origin/feat/a) file2.txt created
004f6a9 file1.txt updated
9e509ac file1.txt created
```

The origin/master points to the latest commit fetched from the remote repository, but it is not reflected on the local master branch yet. To add it into the local branch, we need to merge the local master branch with the origin/master branch:

```
$ git merge origin/master
Updating 5d4eff4..452a918
Fast-forward
 file1.txt | 1 +
 1 file changed, 1 insertion(+)
```

After this point both the local master and origin/master point to the same commit. Let's see the results:

```
$ git log --oneline --all
452a918 (HEAD -> master, origin/master, origin/HEAD) file1.
txt updated
5d4eff4 file1.txt updated
e4f15c0 (origin/feat/a) file2.txt created
004f6a9 file1.txt updated
9e509ac file1.txt created
```

In this example a simple fast-forward was applied to merge two branches. In the following, more complex scenarios are discussed that require other merging techniques.

Note   In applying the fetch command, we need to consider the following:

1.   fetch will not *update* local branches. We need to update our local branches manually.

2.   fetch will not *create* local branches.

Before getting into more complex scenarios, we should note that fetching and merging from remote repositories is a common practice. So Git introduces the pull command as a shortcut that engulfs both fetching and merging operations in a single command (Figure 3-8).

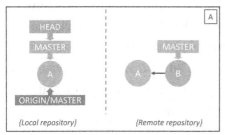 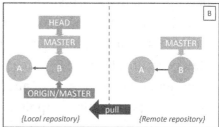

Figure 3-8.   *(A) Remote and local repositories. (B) The pull command fetches and merges the new commit from the remote repository into the local one*

```
$ git pull origin
remote: Enumerating objects: 5, done.
remote: Counting objects: 100% (5/5), done.
remote: Total 3 (delta 0), reused 3 (delta 0), pack-reused 0
Unpacking objects: 100% (3/3), 249 bytes | 35.00 KiB/s, done.
From https://github.com/GitForEng/sample2
   452a918..d63c180  master     -> origin/master
Updating 452a918..d63c180
```

Fast-forward

```
file1.txt | 1 +
1 file changed, 1 insertion(+)
```

Example

Suppose a new commit is inserted on the local master before fetching the remote master. So the origin/master and local master branches are not pointing to the same commit (Figure 3-9 A). After a while other team members push a new commit, let's say "C," into the remote repository (Figure 3-9 B). The commit "C" within the remote repository is pulled onto the origin/master branch. Now, the local master branch and origin/master diverge from each other (Figure 3-9 C). In this situation, a three-way merge is required to incorporate commit "C" into the local master branch. To put it in a nutshell, we fetched "C" from the remote repository onto origin/master. Because of divergence in history lines, we can not directly add "C" into our local master branch; however, we need to create another commit, let's say "D," which is made out of the merge between the local master branch tip point "B" and "C." In the case of divergence, the pull command automatically applies a three-way merge technique.

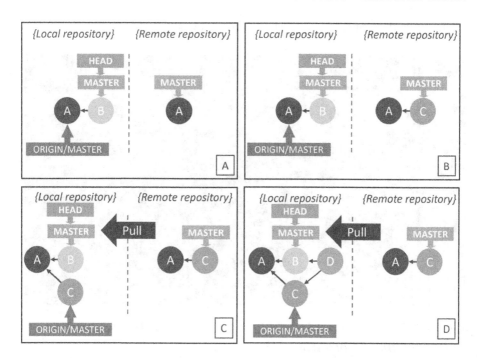

Figure 3-9. *(A) The local master branch is ahead of origin/master. (B) Commit "C" is inserted into the remote repository. (C) Commit "C" is fetched onto origin/master. (D) To make master and origin/master synchronized, a three-way merge is used to create commit D*

```
$ git pull origin
remote: Enumerating objects: 7, done.
remote: Counting objects: 100% (7/7), done.
remote: Compressing objects: 100% (3/3), done.
remote: Total 5 (delta 0), reused 5 (delta 0), pack-reused 0
Unpacking objects: 100% (5/5), 485 bytes | 44.00 KiB/s, done.
From https://github.com/GitForEng/Sample3
   f872b75..278e557  master     -> origin/master
Auto-merging file1.txt
CONFLICT (content): Merge conflict in file1.txt
Automatic merge failed; fix conflicts and then commit the result.
```

To solve the conflict, we call `mergetool` (Figure 3-10).

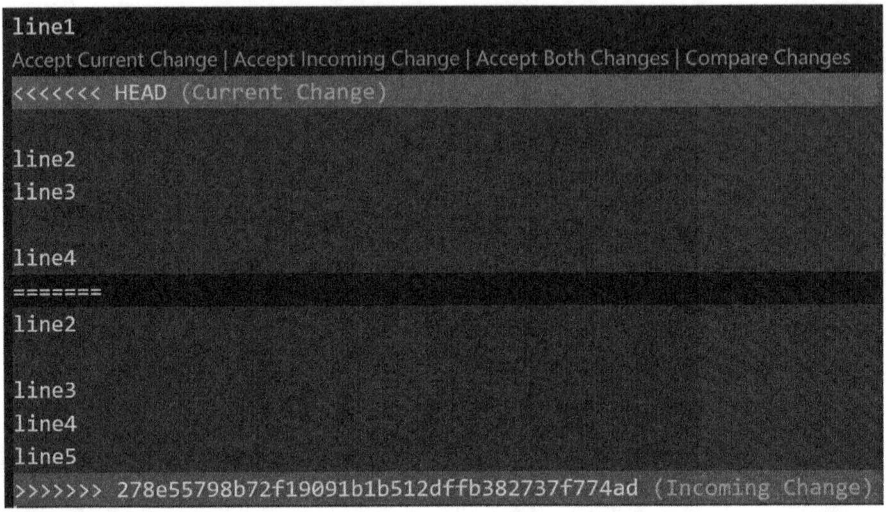

```
line1
Accept Current Change | Accept Incoming Change | Accept Both Changes | Compare Changes
<<<<<<< HEAD (Current Change)

line2
line3

line4
=======
line2

line3
line4
line5
>>>>>>> 278e55798b72f19091b1b512dffb382737f774ad (Incoming Change)
```

Figure 3-10. *mergetool is used to resolve conflicts between master and origin/master branches*

After resolving all conflicts, we need to create a new commit and assign a new commit message (Figure 3-11).

```
Merge branch 'master' of https://github.com/GitForEng/Sample3

# Conflicts:
#     file1.txt
#
# It looks like you may be committing a merge.
# If this is not correct, please run
#     git update-ref -d MERGE_HEAD
# and try again.
```

Figure 3-11. *Assigning a message to the merge commit dialog*

The extra merge commit is not the only option to integrate remote and local branches. Another alternative is rebasing the local `master` branch on `origin/master` (Figure 3-12).

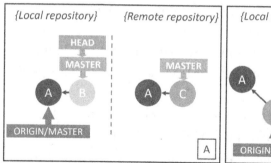
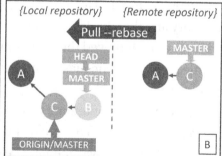

Figure 3-12. *(A) Origin/master is detached from the local master (B). The pull command with the rebase parameter relocates the local master on top of origin/master*

Example

The local master and origin/master branches are detached from each other:

```
$ git log --oneline --all
5661811 (HEAD -> master) file2.txt updated
20e82af (origin/master, origin/HEAD) file1.txt created

$ git pull --rebase origin
remote: Enumerating objects: 5, done.
remote: Counting objects: 100% (5/5), done.
remote: Total 3 (delta 0), reused 3 (delta 0), pack-reused 0
Unpacking objects: 100% (3/3), 244 bytes | 40.00 KiB/s, done.
From https://github.com/GitForEng/Sample4
   20e82af..77ff3d8  master      -> origin/master
Successfully rebased and updated refs/heads/master.

$ git log --oneline --all --graph
* f1ea453 (HEAD -> master) file2.txt updated
* 77ff3d8 (origin/master, origin/HEAD) file1.txt updated
* 20e82af file1.txt created
```

The pull command fetched the 77ff3d8 commit from the remote repository and then inserted it into the origin/master branch, and the rebase parameter moved the master branch on origin/master. In this way, the commit on the master branch, 5661811, is rebased and assigned a new Id f1ea453.

In this example the remote commits had no conflicts with the local ones, but this is not the case all the time! There are situations where we need to apply a three-way merge. The other point we should care about is that the rebase parameter assigns new Ids to the rebased commits. If these commits already exist in the remote repository, changing the commits' Ids would cause confusion and even break the log integrity. For this reason, the rebased pull should only be used on the commits that are not uploaded into a remote repository.

Using the push command, we can prune branches from remote repositories. Calling the push command with the delete parameter, we can eliminate unnecessary branches from the remote repository.

Example

We have three branches – master, feat/a, and bugfix/b1 – in our local repository. Also, we have origin/master, origin/feat/a, and origin/bugfix/b1 branches, which track their corresponding associations:

```
$ git branch --all
  feat/a
  bugfix/b1
* master
  remotes/origin/bugfix/b1
  remotes/origin/feat/a
  remotes/origin/master
```

We need to remove the bugfix/b1 branch from origin:

```
$ git push --delete origin bugfix/b1
From https://github.com/GitForEng/Sample5
 - [deleted]        (none)      -> origin/bugfix/b1
```

This command will remove the `origin/bugfix/b1` branch from our local repository; also, it informs the remote repository to drop out `bugfix/b1`. From this point on, the `bugfix/b1` branch does not exist in the GitHub repository; however, the other contributors need to execute the same command to eliminate their `local origin/bugfix/b1` branches:

```
$ git branch --all
  bugfix/b1
  feat/a
* master
  remotes/origin/feat/a
  remotes/origin/master
```

As we see, the delete parameter removed the `origin/bugfix/b1` branch from the local repository, but the local `bugfix/b1` still exists.

Remote Connections

Using the `remote` command with the --verbose parameter, we can see the remote repository associated with the local clone:

```
$ git remote --verbose
origin  https://github.com/GitForEng/Sample5.git (fetch)
origin  https://github.com/GitForEng/Sample5.git (push)
```

The connection between local and remote repositories is established over two independent channels: one channel transfers data from the remote repository to the local machine, and another channel transfers local data to the remote repository. In this example, the send and receive channels are connected to the same remote repository at `https://github.com/GitForEng/sample5.git`.

Using the remote command, we can assign a different server for the send and receive channels. Three common configurations are shown in Figure 3-13. In the simple form, both channels are connected to the same remote repository (A). In case (B) the fetch and push channels are connected to different repositories. These repositories may be set up on different servers, but their content is the same – otherwise, it will not be possible to keep data consistent. In configuration (C) there are two independent repositories; however, they were assigned to different remote places.

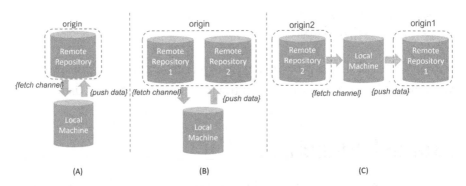

Figure 3-13. *(A) Symmetric connection. All data channels are connected to the same remote repository. (B) Fetch and push channels are differently configured. (C) Fetch and push channels are connected to different remotes*

Using the remote command, we can change the channel's configuration.

To see the assigned remote repositories, we can apply the remote command with the verbose parameter, such as

```
$ git remote --verbose
origin  https://github.com/GitForEng/Sample6-A.git (fetch)
origin  https://github.com/GitForEng/Sample6-A.git (push)
```

To change the address of a remote repository, we can use the remote command with set-url. For example, let's change the url of a remote repository named origin:

```
$ git remote set-url origin https://github.com/
GitForEng/Sample6-B.git
```

Another way is by editing .git/config. We have adjusted our default text editor to Visual Studio Code, and to edit the repository's config file, we call the code command as follows and change the remote repository's address:

```
$ code .git/config
[core]
repositoryformatversion = 0
filemode = true
bare = false
logallrefupdates = true
ignorecase = true
precomposeunicode = true
[remote "origin"]
url = https://github.com/GitForEng/Sample6-B.git
fetch = +refs/heads/feat/a:refs/remotes/origin/feat/a
[branch "feat/a"]
remote = origin
merge = refs/heads/feat/a
```

Let's see the results:

```
$ git remote --verbose
origin  https://github.com/GitForEng/Sample6-B.git (fetch)
origin  https://github.com/GitForEng/Sample6-B.git (push)
```

The command changed both fetch and push channels of origin from Sample6-A to Sample6-B. To change only the push channel, we can use the push parameter like the following:

```
$ git remote set-url --push origin https://github.com/
GitForEng/Sample7.git
```

The result is

```
$ git remote --verbose
origin  https://github.com/GitForEng/Sample6-B.git (fetch)
origin  https://github.com/GitForEng/Sample7.git (push)
```

The fetch channel did not change; however, the push channel is updated. We can associate several remote repositories to a local repository. For example, origin is assigned to Sample6-A, as follows:

```
$ git remote --verbose
origin  https://github.com/GitForEng/Sample6-A.git (fetch)
origin  https://github.com/GitForEng/Sample6-A.git (push)
```

```
$ git remote add origin2 https://github.com/GitForEng/
Sample6-B.git
```

The output is

```
$ git remote --verbose
origin  https://github.com/GitForEng/Sample6-A.git (fetch)
origin  https://github.com/GitForEng/Sample6-A.git (push)
origin2 https://github.com/GitForEng/Sample6-B.git (fetch)
origin2 https://github.com/GitForEng/Sample6-B.git (push)
```

We can remove a remote repository using the remote remove command. For example, let's delete origin2 from the previous example:

```
$ git remote remove origin2
```

The output is

```
$ git remote --verbose
origin  https://github.com/GitForEng/Sample6-A.git (fetch)
origin  https://github.com/GitForEng/Sample6-A.git (push)
```

Example

Cloning a remote repository automatically adds the remote repository to the local clone. In this example, we add an already created remote repository named Sample6-B to a locally initialized repository. We add the remote repository to the local repository using the `remote add` command. This command takes two arguments. The first one is the repository name, and the other one is the repository path:

```
$ git init demo
$ git remote add origin https://github.com/GitForEng/
Sample6-B.git
```

This command adds a remote repository named `origin` with address `https://github.com/GitForEng/Sample6-B.git` to the local repository. Let's see the results:

```
$ git remote --verbose
origin2 https://github.com/GitForEng/Sample6-B.git (fetch)
origin2 https://github.com/GitForEng/Sample6-B.git (push)
```

The remote repository (origin) is associated with the local repository, but we are not finished yet! We need to fetch the remote branches and their commits to the local repository. In this example the remote repository has three branches named `bugfix/a`, `master`, and `feat/a`, and we need all branches to be available in our local repository. Consequently, we use fetch with the `all` parameter:

```
$ git fetch --all
Fetching origin
```

```
remote: Enumerating objects: 28, done.
remote: Counting objects: 100% (28/28), done.
remote: Compressing objects: 100% (14/14), done.
remote: Total 28 (delta 1), reused 28 (delta 1), pack-reused 0
Unpacking objects: 100% (28/28), 2.22 KiB | 42.00 KiB/s, done.
From https://github.com/GitForEng/Sample6-A
 * [new branch]      master     -> origin/master
 * [new branch]      bugfix/a   -> origin/bugfix/a
 * [new branch]      feat/a     -> origin/feat/a
```

The command brings all contents on bugfix/a, feat/a, and master branches into the local repository; however, they are not reflected in the workspace! To see this, let's see the output of the ls command:

```
$ ls
```

It is empty! However, to check the fetch result, we should use the log command:

```
$ git log --all --oneline --graph
* 111a5c0 (origin/bugfix/a) bug.txt created
* 6094084 (origin/master) file1.txt updated
* 843acd7 file1.txt updated
* 8dde2f5 file1.txt updated
| * 53facdf (origin/feat/a) feat.txt updated
| * 6bc3c66 feat.txt updated
| * 6e55b7b feat.txt created
|/
* fe4d54b file1.txt updated
* 6d4f5f4 file1.txt updated
* e4d0d1d file1.txt created
```

The fetch command created origin/bugfix/a, origin/master, and origin/feat/a. These branches are remote tracking branches. However, we need local branches like bugfix/a, master, and feat/a to bring the files received from the remote repository into the workspace. This is achievable by merging the local branches with their remote tracking counterpart, for example, the local master needs to be merged with origin/master. This command automatically creates the master branch and binds it to origin/master:

```
$ git merge origin/master
$ ls
file1.txt
```

Alternatively, we can make tracking branches such as origin/feat/a and origin/bugfix/a without fetching them from a remote repository:

```
$ git checkout --track origin/bugfix/a
Switched to a new branch 'bugfix/a'
Branch 'bugfix/a' set up to track remote branch 'bugfix/a' from
'origin'.
```

```
$ git checkout --track origin/feat/a
Switched to a new branch 'feat/a'
Branch 'feat/a' set up to track remote branch 'feat/a' from
'origin'.
```

Now, all remote branches have their local tracking counterparts in the local repository.

Example

We initiated a new repository using the init command and then added a remote server to it:

```
$ git init demo
```

```
$ git remote add origin https://github.com/GitForEng/
sample1.git
```

Using the pull command, we try to get an exact copy of the remote repository inside the local machine:

```
$ git pull --all
Fetching origin
remote: Enumerating objects: 11, done.
remote: Counting objects: 100% (11/11), done.
remote: Compressing objects: 100% (7/7), done.
remote: Total 11 (delta 0), reused 11 (delta 0), pack-reused 0
Unpacking objects: 100% (11/11), 887 bytes | 55.00 KiB/s, done.
From https://github.com/GitForEng/sample1
 * [new branch]      bugfix/a    -> origin/bugfix/a
 * [new branch]      master      -> origin/master
There is no tracking information for the current branch.
Please specify which branch you want to merge with.
See git-pull(1) for details.

    git pull <remote> <branch>


If you wish to set tracking information for this branch you can
do so with:

    git branch --set-upstream-to=origin/<branch> master
```

The pull command has two phases: first, fetching the remote repository and then merging the current active branch with the remote branches. The message indicates that the fetch operation was successful and all branches were successfully copied into the local machine; however, in the second phase, Git was not successful because it did not know which branch the local master should merge with. We can automate this process such that all the time the local master automatically tracks origin/master. This is achieved by the --set-upstream-to parameter in the branch command:

```
$ git branch --set-upstream-to=origin/master
Branch 'master' set up to track remote branch 'master' from
'origin'.
```

Then, we can pull all branches without an issue:

```
$ git pull --all
Fetching origin
Already up to date.
```

We can get more information about local and remote branches using the branch command followed by the very verbose parameter:

```
$ git branch -vv
* master 7ac4b18 [origin/master] file3.txt created
```

Example

An empty repository is initialized in GitHub, and a fresh repository is constructed in the local machine. The remote repository address is added to the local repository. A few commits are submitted into the local repository. When these commits are pushed to the remote repository

```
$ git init demo09
$ git remote add origin https://github.com/GitForEng/
Sample7.git
```

```
$ git push origin
fatal: The current branch master has no upstream branch.
To push the current branch and set the remote as upstream, use

    git push --set-upstream origin master
```

Git complains about a nonexisting branch. This is because a fresh remote repository does not have any branch in it yet. If we want to push our local branch, for example, master, to a remote repository, we need to have the tracking branch on the remote storage already. To make a new branch in an empty GitHub using the push command, we can use the --set-upstream parameter like

```
$ git push --set-upstream origin master
Enumerating objects: 6, done.
Counting objects: 100% (6/6), done.
Delta compression using up to 16 threads
Compressing objects: 100% (2/2), done.
Writing objects: 100% (6/6), 453 bytes | 453.00 KiB/s, done.
Total 6 (delta 0), reused 0 (delta 0), pack-reused 0
To https://github.com/GitForEng/Sample7.git
 * [new branch]      master -> master
Branch 'master' set up to track remote branch 'master' from
'origin'.
```

The set-upstream parameter informs Git to construct a master branch (if it is not already existing) in the origin repository.

Race Condition

In a multiclient environment, it is possible to have multiple clients that want to push their local branches to the remote repository at the same time. Consider Figure 3-14 A. Inside the remote repository, there are only commits "A" and "B." We have commits "A," "B," and "C" in our local branch. The local master branch and the remote master branch are linearly accessible. In other words, it is possible to merge them using a simple fast-forward merge. However, before we send our local commits, someone else pushes commit "D" to the remote repository (Figure 3-14 B).

In this situation the remote master branch is not consistent with our local branch. One method for pushing our master branch to the remote branch is to apply the force parameter. This is a solution that one should never apply because forceful push overwrites the other clients' contributions (Figure 3-14 C).

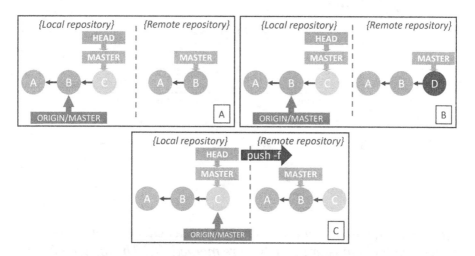

Figure 3-14. *(A) A new commit is stored in the local repository. (B) Before pushing local commits into the remote repository, a new commit "D" is received into the remote repository. (C) The push command with the force parameter causes the local commit "C" to overwrite the remote commit D*

The other method is to fetch the remote repository content (Figure 3-15 A). In this way, we assure the other team members' contribution is available in our local repository. Then, we merge the latest received commits with our local branch (Figure 3-15 B). Finally, we push the updates to the remote repository (Figure 3-15 C). You may notice that at the beginning the objective was to push only the "C" commit, but after merge, we pushed two commits: "E" and "C."

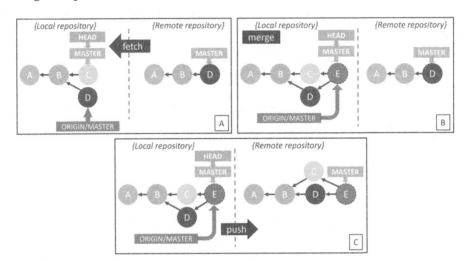

Figure 3-15. *(A) The remote repository is fetched. (B) The origin/ master and local master branches are merged. (C) The local commits are pushed*

Example

We make a new commit into the local repository and then try to push it to the remote repository. Our request is rejected:

```
$ git log --oneline --all
f4761e1 (HEAD -> master) file1.txt updated
a79204d Merge branch 'master' of https://github.com/
GitForEng/Sample3
278e557 (origin/master, origin/HEAD) file2.txt updated
3601b19 file1.txt updated
0f9383c file1.txt updated
f872b75 file1.txt updated
```

```
$ git push origin
To https://github.com/GitForEng/Sample3.git
 ! [rejected]          master -> master (fetch first)
error: failed to push some refs to 'https://github.com/
GitForEng/Sample3.git'
hint: Updates were rejected because the remote contains work
that you do
hint: not have locally. This is usually caused by another
repository pushing
hint: to the same ref. You may want to first integrate the
remote changes
hint: (e.g., 'git pull ...') before pushing again.
hint: See the 'Note about fast-forwards' in 'git push --help'
for details.
```

To solve this error, we need to fetch the remote repository

```
$ git fetch origin
remote: Enumerating objects: 5, done.
remote: Counting objects: 100% (5/5), done.
remote: Compressing objects: 100% (2/2), done.
remote: Total 3 (delta 0), reused 3 (delta 0), pack-reused 0
Unpacking objects: 100% (3/3), 281 bytes | 56.00 KiB/s, done.
From https://github.com/GitForEng/Sample3
   278e557..1cf0602  master      -> origin/master
```

and then merge it with the local master:

```
$ git merge origin/master
Auto-merging file1.txt
CONFLICT (content): Merge conflict in file1.txt
Automatic merge failed; fix conflicts and then commit
the result.
```

If a conflict happens, we can use mergetool (Figure 3-16):

```
$ git mergetool
```

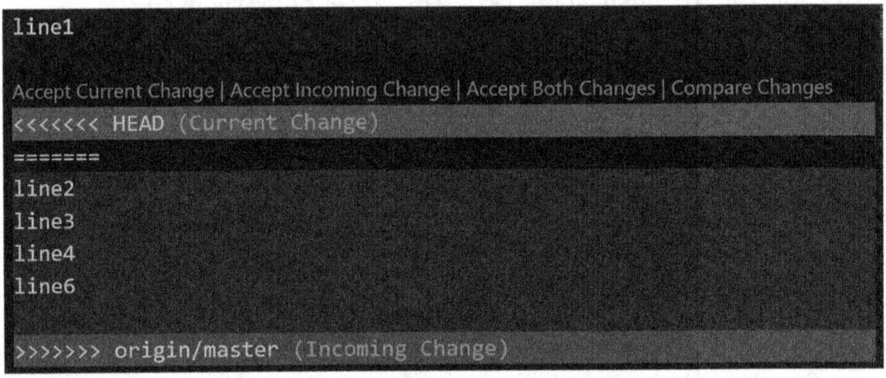

```
line1

Accept Current Change | Accept Incoming Change | Accept Both Changes | Compare Changes
<<<<<<< HEAD (Current Change)
=======
line2
line3
line4
line6

>>>>>>> origin/master (Incoming Change)
```

Figure 3-16. *mergetool is used to resolve local and remote merge conflicts*

The merge conflicts are resolved, and we continue with the merge process (Figure 3-17):

```
$ git merge --continue
```

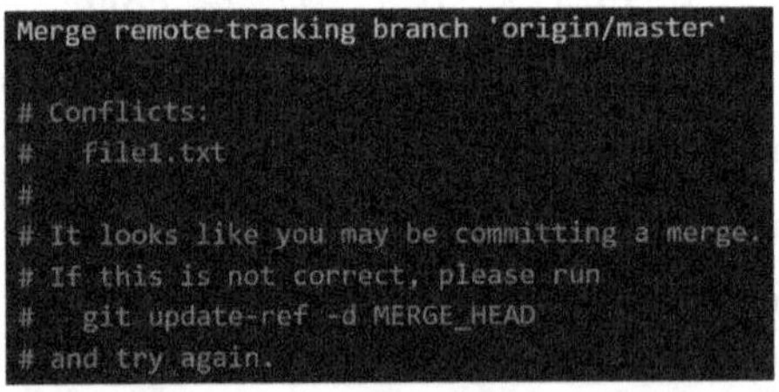

```
Merge remote-tracking branch 'origin/master'

# Conflicts:
#	file1.txt
#
# It looks like you may be committing a merge.
# If this is not correct, please run
#	git update-ref -d MERGE_HEAD
# and try again.
```

Figure 3-17. *Creating a new commit after resolving all conflicts between remote and local master branches*

Now we can push the local master branch to the remote repository (Figure 3-18).

```
MINGW64 (master)
$ git log --oneline --all --graph
*   91d93f3 (HEAD -> master, origin/master) Merge remote-tracking branch 'origin/master'
|\
| *   44928b2 Merge remote-tracking branch 'origin/master'
| |\
| * | f4761e1 file1.txt updated
| * | a79204d Merge branch 'master' of https://github.com/GitForEng/Sample3
| |\|
| * | | 0f9383c file1.txt updated
|* | | 7bcb550 file1.txt updated
|* | | c02b4ab file1.txt updated file2.txt deleted file3.txt created
|/| /
| * | | 1cf0602 file1.txt updated
| |/
|/|
|* | 278e557 file2.txt updated
|* | 3601b19 file1.txt updated
|/
* f872b75 file1.txt updated
```

Figure 3-18. *Log history after successfully merging remote and local master branches*

Tags and Releases

Tags are useful to mark some special commits. Usually these commits contain *released* versions of the product. When GitHub receives a tagged commit, it automatically encapsulates the contents of that commit into a zip file. So users can independently download a released commit, without a need to store the rest of the history line.

Example

Suppose the last commit we submitted into our local repository is version 1.0 of our project. We can tag this commit as V1.0 like this

```
$ git tag V1.0
```

The string V1.0 is an arbitrary name that we want to call our released version. The name is not a formatted string, but it cannot contain any of the \, ?, ~, ^, :, *, [, @, and space characters. If the released version is behind HEAD, then we can use relative addressing such as

```
$ git tag V0.7 HEAD~1
```

or we can use an absolute commit Id to tag it. For example, let's mark a commit with the 0627738 Id:

```
$ git tag V0.1 0627738
```

We can see the list of tags using the -l parameter:

```
$ git tag -l
```

The push command does not transfer tags. For this, we can directly specify which tag should be pushed

```
$ git push origin V1.0
```

or we can push all tags at once:

```
$ git push --tag origin
Total 0 (delta 0), reused 0 (delta 0), pack-reused 0
To https://github.com/GitForEng/Sample7.git
 * [new tag]         V0.1 -> V0.1
 * [new tag]         V0.7 -> V0.7
 * [new tag]         V1.0 -> V1.0
```

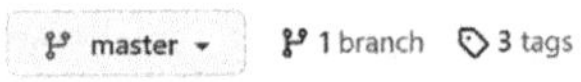

⌥ master ▾   ⌥ 1 branch   ◇ 3 tags

Figure 3-19. *All tags are uploaded to the remote repositories*

Now, if we check the remote repository inside the Tags section we can find the zip files (Figure 3-20).

Figure 3-20. *Tags are encapsulated as zip files. Each zip file is separately available and directly downloaded*

In the release mode we can download a released version.

Figure 3-21. *GitHub encapsulates the contents of a tagged commit inside a zip file. These files are directly accessible out of the log history*

To remove a tag inside the remote repository, we can use the delete parameter:

```
$ git push origin --delete V0.1
To https://github.com/GitForEng/Sample7.git
 - [deleted]         V0.1
```

Merge Independent Repositories

Alice and Bob started to work on a project. They have developed the project independent of each other at the beginning, but later on they decide to share their contributions with each other. So Alice constructs an empty remote repository in GitHub and pushes her master branch to it (Figure 3-22).

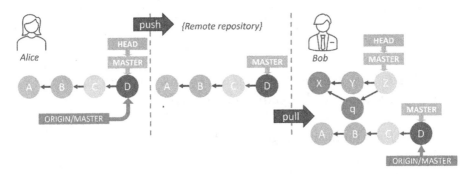

Figure 3-22. *Alice and Bob started from different initial contents. Alice pushed her commits to the remote repository, and Bob pulled them. Bob's local repository has two independent trees*

Then Bob pulls Alice's contributions into his local machine:

```
$ git pull origin
```

Bob reformats the commits by authors (Figure 3-23):

```
$ git log --all --graph --pretty=format:"%h %an %s"
```

```
$ git log --all --graph --pretty=format:"%h   %an      %s"
* 1a6e94f  Bob     File1.txt updated
* 532ce77  Bob     File1.txt created
* 70f2682  Alice    File1.txt updated
* bb9758d  Alice    File1.txt created
```

Figure 3-23. *Bob checks which commit is submitted by Alice and which one is submitted by himself*

In the format string, the first placeholder "%h" stands for hash code, "%an" is the author name, and "%s" is the subject of the commit. You should notice the pull command did not complain about irrelevant history lines. Indeed, Git downloads the remote repository contents beside the local contents. In other words, we have two independent trees in a single repository (Figure 3-24).

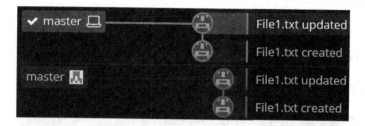

Figure 3-24. *Two independent log trees in a single repository*

Now, Bob decides to merge Alice's commits with his own commits (Figure 3-25):

```
$ git merge origin/master
```

Figure 3-25. *Bob failed to merge two independent trees*

The merge command refuses to merge unrelated histories. Bob is sure that this merge is not harmful; so he enforces the merge to continue with the allow-unrelated-histories parameter:

```
$ git merge --allow-unrelated-histories origin/master
```

```
MINGW64  (master)
$ git merge --allow-unrelated-histories origin/master
CONFLICT (add/add): Merge conflict in File1.txt
Auto-merging File1.txt
Automatic merge failed; fix conflicts and then commit the result.

MINGW64  (master|MERGING)
$ git mergetool File1.txt
```

Figure 3-26. *The allow-unrelated-histories option lets two independent trees to be merged*

Then, to resolve the conflicts, Bob uses the default merge tool (Figure 3-27):

```
$ git mergetool File1.txt
```

```
Line1
Accept Current Change | Accept Incoming Change | Accept Both Changes | Compare Changes
<<<<<<< HEAD (Current Change)

Line2

Line3
Line4
=======
>>>>>>> origin/master (Incoming Change)
```

Figure 3-27. *Merging two independent trees follows the same steps applied for merging on one tree*

After resolving the conflicts, Bob continues with the merging:

```
$ git merge --continue
```

The final status of Bob's repository is shown in Figure 3-28.

```
MINGW64  (master)
$ git log --all --oneline --graph
*   0a75569 (HEAD -> master) Merge remote-tracking branch 'origin/master'
|\
| * 70f2682 (origin/master) File1.txt updated
| * bb9758d File1.txt created
* 1a6e94f File1.txt updated
* 532ce77 File1.txt created
```

Figure 3-28. *Two independent trees are fused at the merge commit*

Fork

In scaled projects, like Linux kernel, not all developers are allowed to directly manipulate the original repository. This is since a buggy or malfunctioning contribution from an unknown source is potentially riskful and can collapse the entire or part of the project.

In these types of projects, a team of maintainers let contributors make a copy of the project for themselves (in their own accounts), which is called *fork*. Then contributors start to work on their fork. When they are finished with their tasks, they send a push request to the maintainers to evaluate their fork. The request is evaluated, and if it is approved, the contributions are integrated into the original project repository.

Example

SyncBox is an open source medical motherboard that we want to add a readme.txt document to. First, we need to find it in GitHub (Figure 3-29).

Figure 3-29. *Using the GitHub search bar, we can find the repository we need*

Sometimes many results may show up for a single search. Among the results, we select the repository we need (Figure 3-30).

Figure 3-30. *SyncBox source repository on GitHub*

Inside the repository, there is a Fork option. By clicking the Fork button, we will have our own local copy (Figure 3-31).

Figure 3-31. *The Fork option creates a new fork from the repository*

We clone the forked repository on our local machine:

```
$ git clone --branch master --single-branch https://github.com/
GitForEng/syncbox.git syncbox
```

Then we add readme.txt.

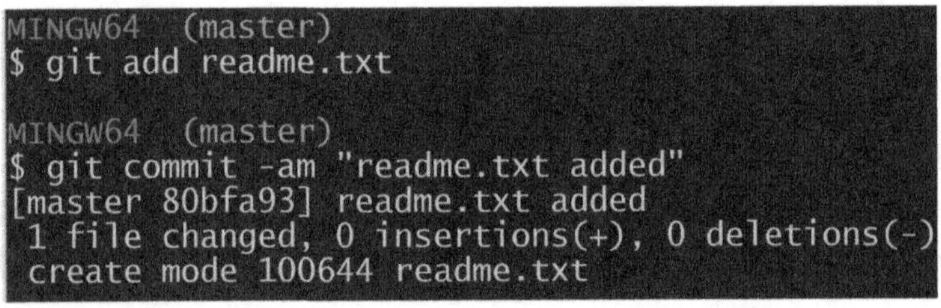

```
MINGW64  (master)
$ git add readme.txt

MINGW64  (master)
$ git commit -am "readme.txt added"
[master 80bfa93] readme.txt added
 1 file changed, 0 insertions(+), 0 deletions(-)
 create mode 100644 readme.txt
```

Figure 3-32. *Readme.txt added into the local repository*

Now we push the local repository to our forked repository:

```
$ git push origin
```

Within our GitHub account, we switch to Pull requests (Figure 3-33).

Figure 3-33. *Pull requests is selected in the forked repository*

By clicking the "New pull request" button, a new pull request sequence is initiated. First, a summary of the updates are shown (Figure 3-34).

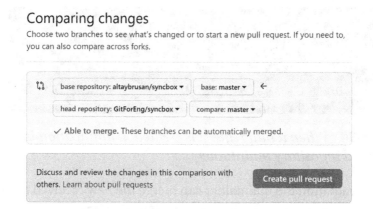

Figure 3-34. *Pull request starts by a summary of the source and destination of the request*

Then we click "Create pull request" to send the request (Figure 3-35).

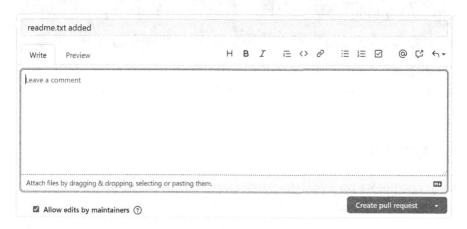

Figure 3-35. *Pull request form*

We can put a note for the maintainers and send the request. The maintainers would see the notification (Figure 3-36).

Figure 3-36. *When a pull request is created, a notification is sent to the original repository maintainers*

After evaluation the maintainer can merge the new received request into the original data repository or reject it (Figure 3-37).

Figure 3-37. *Maintainers could accept the pull request and integrate the newly arrived contributions into the source repository*

Summary

In this chapter we reviewed the remote repository connection and management methods. A summary of methods that we reviewed is as follows:

```
git clone [address] [destination]
git clone --branch feat/a --single-branch [address] [dest]

git branch --remote
git branch --all
```

```
git push [remote repo]
git push [remote repo] --delete [tag]
git push [remote repo] [tag]
git push [remote repo] [branch]
git push --all [remote repo]
git push --delete [remote repo] [branch]
git push --set-upstream [remote repo] [branch]
git push --tag [remote repo]

git fetch [remote repo]
git fetch --all

git pull [remote repo]
git pull [remote repo][branch]

git pull --rebase [remote repo]
git pull --prune [remote repo]
git remote --verbose
git remote set-url [remote repo] [address]
git remote set-url --push [remote repo] [address]
git remote add [remote repo] [address]
git remote remove [remote repo]
git remote add [remote repo] [address]
git checkout --track [remote branch]
git branch --set-upstream-to=[remote branch]
git branch --vv

git tag [tag name]
git tag [tag name] [commit Id]

  git merge --allow-unrelated-histories [remote branch]
```

CHAPTER 4

Commit Reforming

Commits contain tangible units of progress toward the project's goal. Each commit is indeed a pace in the project road map. In the ideal world, all commits are self-sufficient and do not require any modification after they are submitted into a repository. However, in the real world, this is not the case all the time! For example, after submitting we may find the commit message is not clear enough or it does not include all pieces of information. For such situations, Git envisioned a list of actions to update history:

- Squash small commits.

- Split large commits.

- Reword commit messages.

- Drop unwanted commits.

- Modify commits.

Published commits should never be rewritten or changed because it could damage the other contributors' history line (Figure 4-1).

© Altay Brusan and Aytac Durmaz 2022
A. Brusan and A. Durmaz, *Git for Electronic Circuit Design*, Maker Innovations Series,
https://doi.org/10.1007/978-1-4842-8124-6_4

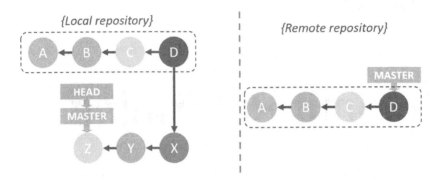

Figure 4-1. *Published commits {A,B,C,D} are shared between all team members and should not be modified. Local commits {X,Y,Z} are open to manipulate*

Note   Techniques that are introduced in this chapter should only apply on local commits that have not been shared with the other team members.

Reflog Command

The log command is a handy tool to list the history of a repository. It provides a variety of information about commits such as the branch, author, date/time, etc. However, the log command does not consider orphaned commits or pruned branches. Deleted branches and commits are not erased from disk immediately. They exist on disk for a while, but they are not accessible. In this period, we can rescue them. To access deleted items, we can use reflog. It shows the trace of the tips of all branches in the course of time.

Example

Suppose three commits are added into the local repository. The `reflog` command output is

```
$ git reflog
7f52363 (HEAD -> master) HEAD@{0}: commit: file1.txt updated
b5f0639 HEAD@{1}: commit: file1.txt updated
bad0180 HEAD@{2}: commit (initial): file1.txt created
```

The output of the log command is

```
$ git log --oneline
7f52363 (HEAD -> master) file1.txt updated
b5f0639 file1.txt updated
bad0180 file1.txt created
```

Each line of the reflog result starts with the commit Id associated with HEAD. HEAD@{n} means the position of the HEAD pointer at the nth commit before the last. For example, at HEAD@{1} (in other notation, HEAD~1), the head was pointing to commit b5f0639. Now, we apply a hard reset and compare the log and reflog outputs:

```
$ git reflog
b5f0639 (HEAD -> master) HEAD@{0}: reset: moving to HEAD~1
7f52363 HEAD@{1}: commit: file1.txt updated
b5f0639 (HEAD -> master) HEAD@{2}: commit: file1.txt updated
bad0180 HEAD@{3}: commit (initial): file1.txt created
```

```
$ git log --oneline
b5f0639 (HEAD -> master) file1.txt updated
bad0180 file1.txt created
```

Suppose sometime later we find that we mistakenly reseted the commit and we need to return it back. For this, we need the hard-reseted commit Id. The log command does not provide any information about the reseted (deleted) commits and branches. However, reflog provides this information. From the reflog results, we notice at HEAD@{0} a reset happens and HEAD is moved to HEAD~1 (a commit with Id b5f0639). But before that point, reflog was on commit with Id 7f52363. This is the deleted commit Id. We can not get to this Id using the log command. Let's revert the reset command:

```
$ git reset --hard 7f52363
HEAD is now at 7f52363 file1.txt updated
```

This command returns the 7f52363 commit back to the log.

Garbage Collection

Git has a garbage collector tool that is responsible for cleaning the orphaned or unreachable commits. It is automatically called after special commands such as pull, merge, and rebase. Nevertheless, the housekeeping does not get into action immediately. It starts after a timer is triggered. This is because Git wants to give the user the chance to recover the mistakes.

The trigger period of the garbage collector timer is sufficient for usual projects; however, we can customize it for our own specifications. In the following we will see an example of how to tune the garbage collector timer.

Example
The "reflogExpireUnreachable" parameter of gc defines how often a non-accessible reflog entry output should be deleted:

```
$ git config gc.reflogExpireUnreachable now
```

This command adjusts the garbage collector (gc) to immediately remove inaccessible reflog entries after the cleanup process. With this format, the update is applied on the current repository only; however, to make the change for all repositories, we should add the `--global` parameter. To see how it works, let's trace the output of the reflog before and after the cleanup process. Before making any change on the current repository, the reflog is like

```
$ git reflog
d7d808b (HEAD -> master) HEAD@{0}: commit: file1.txt updated
54b8010 HEAD@{1}: commit: file1.txt updated
11dd8a9 HEAD@{2}: commit: file1.txt updated
de49853 HEAD@{3}: commit (initial): file1.txt created
```

To make an unreachable commit, we reset the repository to HEAD~1, so the last commit is no longer accessible:

```
$ git reset --hard HEAD~1
```

We force the garbage collector to start the cleaning operation:

```
$ git gc
Enumerating objects: 9, done.
Counting objects: 100% (9/9), done.
Delta compression using up to 16 threads
Compressing objects: 100% (3/3), done.
Writing objects: 100% (9/9), done.
Total 9 (delta 0), reused 0 (delta 0), pack-reused 0
```

Now we check reflog:

```
$ git reflog
54b8010 (HEAD -> master) HEAD@{0}: commit: file1.txt updated
11dd8a9 HEAD@{1}: commit: file1.txt updated
de49853 HEAD@{2}: commit (initial): file1.txt created
```

After the cleanup process, the inaccessible commit, d7d808b, is deleted from the reflog history.

Amend the Last Commit

We can change the *last* commit's message through the amend parameter. Suppose in the last commit we made a typo in the commit message, but before committing anything else, we noticed the error:

```
$ git log --oneline
8e12818 (HEAD -> master) file1.txt updted
5c94b00 file1.txt updated
```

To solve the problem, we can use the commit command with the --amend parameter like

```
$ git commit --amend -m "file1.txt updated"
[master 0aac740] file1.txt updated
 Date: Mon Nov 8 12:21:06 2021 +0300
 1 file changed, 1 insertion(+)
```

After the update we would have the following structure:

```
$ git log --oneline
0aac740 (HEAD -> master) file1.txt updated
5c94b00 file1.txt updated
c391ce6 file1.txt updated
```

One should notice the Id of the amended commit is changed. Indeed, Git created a new commit with a new Id and assigned the new message to it. As there is no commit in front of the last amended commit, this operation is not harmful.

Example

In this example, suppose we need to change the contents of the last commit:

```
$ git diff --stat HEAD~1..HEAD
 file1.txt | 1 +
 file2.txt | 0
 2 files changed, 1 insertion(+)
```

In this commit one insertion is made on file1.txt, and a new empty file2.txt is created. Before adding any new commit, we notice that file2.txt should not be included in this commit, and we need to take it out. We start with resetting the last commit with the mixed parameter:

```
$ git reset --mixed HEAD~1
Unstaged changes after reset:
M       file1.txt
```

At this point the status of the repository is like

```
$ git status
On branch master
Changes not staged for commit:
  (use "git add <file>..." to update what will be committed)
  (use "git restore <file>..." to discard changes in working
  directory)
        modified:   file1.txt

Untracked files:
  (use "git add <file>..." to include in what will be committed)
        file2.txt

no changes added to commit (use "git add" and/or "git
commit -a")
```

The reset command cancels the changes in the last commit and moves the HEAD pointer to one commit back. Consequently, file2.txt is untracked because it was added into the stage area at the last commit. Also, file1.txt inside the stage area is one version behind the workspace, so it is marked as modified. Now, we can split files into two separate commits such that file1.txt appears in one commit and file2.txt is stored inside the next one (Figure 4-2).

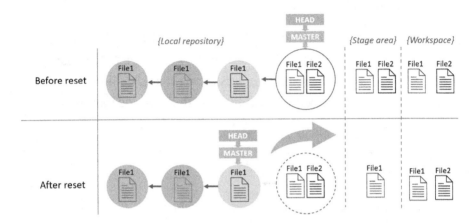

Figure 4-2. *After reset with the "mixed" parameter, the contents of the stage area and HEAD location are updated*

Let's store file1.txt in a separate commit:

```
$ git add file1.txt
warning: LF will be replaced by CRLF in file1.txt.
The file will have its original line endings in your working
directory

$ git commit -m "file1.txt updated"
[master 65e8198] file1.txt updated
 1 file changed, 1 insertion(+)
```

For file2.txt, we make a new commit and add it into that commit:

```
$ git add .
$ git commit -m "file2.txt created"
[master 36bc2b7] file2.txt created
 1 file changed, 0 insertions(+), 0 deletions(-)
 create mode 100644 file2.txt
```

Amend a Middle Commit

The last commit on a branch is a special one. We can change it without causing any problem for the rest of the commits on the branch. In the following we will see how we can amend a commit other than the last one.

Example

There are a couple of commits in the repository. file1.txt and file2.txt are updated in each of them:

```
$ git log --oneline
871f217 (HEAD -> master) file1 file2 updated
b574cdf file2.txt updates
96dd0e9 file2.txt created
0d29dab file1 updated
5847c65 file1.txt created
```

We need to change the commit "96dd0e9." We start the amendment with rebasing from the parent of the commit:

```
$ git rebase -i 0d29dab
```

Here, -i stands for interactive. The command opens the To-Do list editor (Figure 4-3). In this menu, we can apply different rebasing commands on each commit.

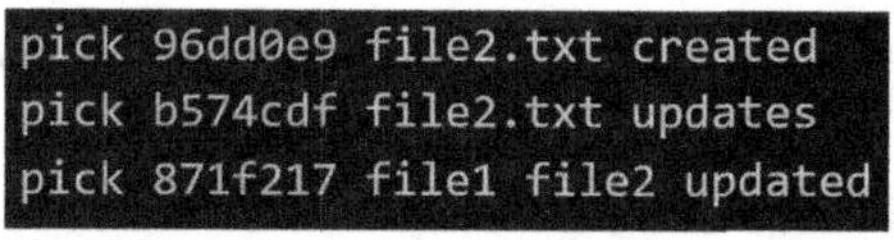

```
pick 96dd0e9 file2.txt created
pick b574cdf file2.txt updates
pick 871f217 file1 file2 updated
```

Figure 4-3. *The rebase To-Do list menu. The syntax is as follows: (i) command name, (ii) commit Id, (iii) commit message*

Each line represents the action to be done on the corresponding commit, such that the first word is the command name, the second one is the short hash Id of the commit, and the last part is the commit's message. For each commit there are a couple of commands we can apply. A subset of these commands is shown in Table 4-1.

Table 4-1. *Short list of commands that are applicable on each commit in interactive rebasing*

Command	Description
pick	Try to use the commit as is.
reword	Only update the commit message.
edit	Amend the commit.
squash	Join the commit with the previous one.
drop	Delete the commit.

In this example we only need to *edit* the 96dd0e9 commit and pick the other ones intact (Figure 4-4).

```
edit 96dd0e9 file2.txt created
pick b574cdf file2.txt updates
pick 871f217 file1 file2 updated
```

Figure 4-4. *The edit command is applied on commit 96dd0e9*

After updating the To-Do list, we need to save the changes and close the editor. In the Bash environment, Git receives the To-Do list and starts to execute the selected command on each commit (Figure 4-5).

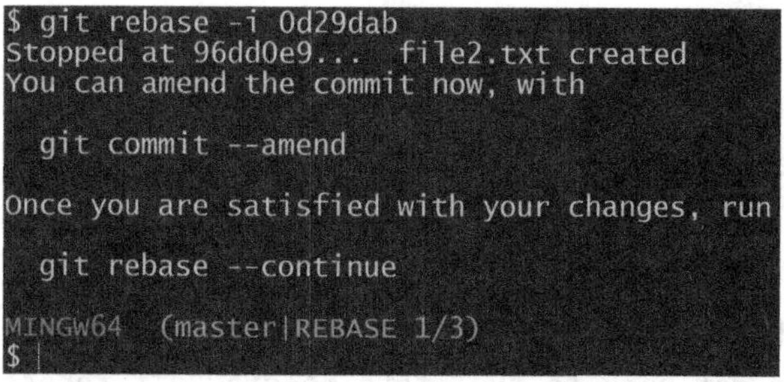

Figure 4-5. *For each commit on the branch then, the rebase process applies the changes. We need to resolve the potential conflicts*

Git starts to apply the To-Do list line by line. The first command is editing 96dd0e9. We update file1.txt in the workspace, add it into the stage area, and then commit it into the local repository:

```
$ git add file1.txt
$ git commit --amend -m "file1.txt amended"
[detached HEAD 96ac91d] file1.txt amended
 Date: Tue Nov 9 08:12:12 2021 +0300
 2 files changed, 8 insertions(+)
 create mode 100644 file2.txt
```

We have finished with the first commit. Now, three options are available. First, return to edit mode (Figure 4-6):

```
$ git rebase --edit-todo
```

Figure 4-6. *Edit the To-Do list with the remaining commits*

The second option is to cancel the rebasing operation:

```
$ git rebase --abort
```

The third option is to continue with the rebasing of the next commit:

```
$ git rebase --continue
error: could not apply 871f217... file1 file2 updated
Resolve all conflicts manually, mark them as resolved with
"git add/rm <conflicted_files>", then run "git rebase --continue".
You can instead skip this commit: run "git rebase --skip".
To abort and get back to the state before "git rebase", run
"git rebase --abort".
Could not apply 871f217... file1 file2 updated
Auto-merging file1.txt
CONFLICT (content): Merge conflict in file1.txt
MINGW64  (master|REBASE 3/3)
```

We have updated file1.txt in the 96dd0e9 commit. In the b574cdf commit, file1.txt is not changed. However, in the 871f217 commit, file1.txt is changed. The changes we made in the 96dd0e9 commit are in conflict with the changes stored in 871f217. So we need to solve this issue:

```
$ git mergetool file1.txt
```

After solving the conflicts, we need to add the file and commit it:

```
$ git add file1.txt
$ git commit -m "file1.txt updated"
```

At this point we can reopen the To-Do list again, abort the rebasing, or continue with the rebasing:

```
$ git rebase --continue
```

The rebase operation rebuilds commits. We can check this with the log command:

```
$ git log --oneline
9b38edf (HEAD -> master) file1.txt updated
88cb11b file2.txt updates
```

```
96ac91d file1.txt amended
0d29dab file1 updated
5847c65 file1.txt created
```

Rewording a Commit Message

Sometimes the commit messages are not self-explanatory, or a typo happens. In this situation we can update commit messages by means of the rebase command.

Example

We found a typo has happened in a commit message:

```
$ git log --oneline
183b79e (HEAD -> master) file1.txt updated
638e402 file1.txt updated
766c69f file1.txt updted
4472c17 file1.txt updated
5352980 file1.txt created
```

Using the rebase command, we edit the To-Do list and add the "reword" command to the target commit (Figure 4-7):

```
$ git rebase -i 4472c17
```

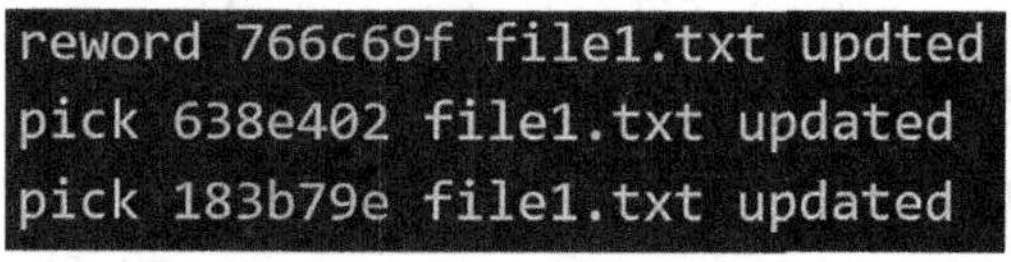

```
reword 766c69f file1.txt updted
pick 638e402 file1.txt updated
pick 183b79e file1.txt updated
```

Figure 4-7. *The reword command is applied on the target commit*

After closing the To-Do list, the commit message editing window opens. We can update the log message and save the changes. The final output is

```
$ git log --oneline
41c1b72 (HEAD -> master) file1.txt updated
058b62d file1.txt updated
05b5c82 file1.txt updated
4472c17 file1.txt updated
5352980 file1.txt created
```

You should notice that the commit Ids after the reworded commit are recreated.

Change the Commit Order

We can change the order of commits on a branch. To do this, we need to change the commit order in the To-Do list of the rebase command.

Example

Suppose there are four independent commits in the local repository that have no conflicts with each other. We need to reorder all commits in between second and the last one on the branch:

```
$ git log --oneline
b18dbd4 (HEAD -> master) file4.txt created
4e3852e file3.txt created
05a9c8d file2.txt created
d501c4f file1.txt created
```

We call the rebase command and open the To-Do list. Inside the list, we rearrange the commits as follows (Figure 4-8).

```
pick b18dbd4 file4.txt created
pick 4e3852e file3.txt created
pick 05a9c8d file2.txt created
```

Figure 4-8. *Commits are reordered. The 05a9c8d and b18dbd4 commit orders are exchanged with each other*

Let's check the results after closing the To-Do list:

```
$ git log --oneline
a070aca (HEAD -> master) file2.txt created
5d71c5a file3.txt created
f00fbb9 file4.txt created
d501c4f file1.txt created
```

In this example commits were independent of each other. If there were conflicts, then Git would stop the rebasing process and ask for resolving them. In this situation we can use mergetool to handle the conflicts.

The first commit on a branch has no parent. For this reason, the rebase command cannot change its order. To change the first commit's order, we need to add an empty commit before it and rewrite the history such that the empty commit comes after the first commit. This operation does not fit into the best practice guidelines because it may change the commits' authors. In real applications it is preferred to have only a satellite document such as a readme file inside the first commit. So there would be no need to change the commit's location in the future.

Combine Commits

Using the rebase command, we can combine multiple commits in one.

Example

There are four independent commits inside the local repository. The last two commits are too small, and we need to combine them into each other. First, the rebase tool is invoked:

```
$ git log --oneline
34e78bd (HEAD -> master) file4.txt created
b65cfc0 file3.txt created
5f9292a file2.txt created
6164388 file1.txt created
```

The command for the last commit is changed to squash (Figure 4-9). This command combines the last commit into the previous one:

```
$ git rebase -i 5f9292a
```

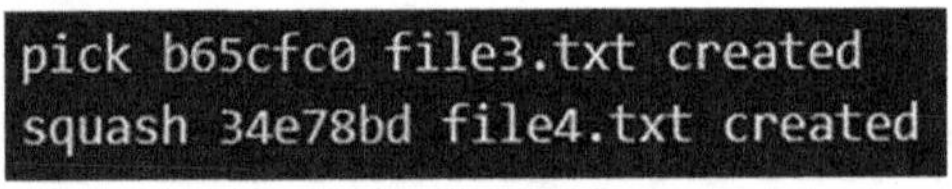

```
pick b65cfc0 file3.txt created
squash 34e78bd file4.txt created
```

Figure 4-9. *The squash command in front of a commit merges it with the previous commit*

When the To-Do list is closed, the new commit message editor shows up (Figure 4-10).

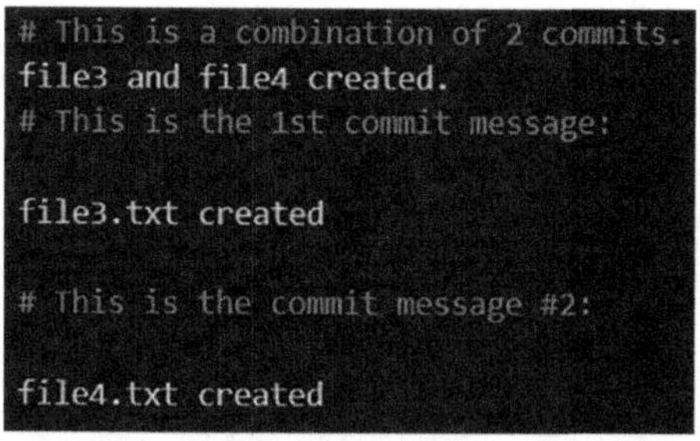

Figure 4-10. A new commit is made out of two squashed ones

We changed the commits, and the final output is

```
$ git log --oneline
3e603e6 (HEAD -> master) file3 and file4 created.
5f9292a file2.txt created
6164388 file1.txt created
```

Summary

In this chapter we reviewed common commands used for reorganizing the commits on the branches. We have discussed that the last commit on a branch is somewhat different from the rest of the commits. We can manipulate it with no harm to the rest of the commits on the branch. Making a change to the other commits is also possible, but we should notice that this will recreate them:

```
$ git reflog
$ git config gc.reflogExpireUnreachable now
$ git gc
$ git commit --amend -m "file1.txt updated"
$ git gc
$ git rebase -i 0d29dab
$ git rebase --abort
$ git rebase --continue
$ git rebase --continue
```

CHAPTER 5

Managing a Circuit Design Project

As no success is achieved by chance, to accomplish a circuit design project, an established development workflow is mandatory. A well-designed workflow provides a pathway toward success and helps us avoid falling into the trap of divergences. A workflow provides answers to the following questions:

- What are the tasks to be done?

- What is the order of the tasks?

- What are the time intervals of each task?

- Who is responsible for accomplishing each task?

- What are the achievements (results) of each task?

- How are the task results prepared?

- What are the acceptance criteria for each task?

- What are the risks and mitigation plans?

- How to evaluate achievements?

Besides workflow we also need tools to help us with managing the project artifacts. In the software development ecosystem, there are a wide range of workflows (such as Agile methodologies) and tools (kanban

© Altay Brusan and Aytac Durmaz 2022
A. Brusan and A. Durmaz, *Git for Electronic Circuit Design*, Maker Innovations Series,
https://doi.org/10.1007/978-1-4842-8124-6_5

boards, development environments, etc.) available that are useful for tracing the steps, times, and monitoring the achievements. We can apply these methods and tools for electrical circuit design projects. In this chapter, we will use Git as a basic tool that provides managers with feedback from the project progress. Managers, by looking at the commit timeline, could track the project progress. But, before diving into the details, first, we will review a workspace structure for a well-structured electrical project categorization. This structure provides a standardized organization for the project's contents. Then we review two basic project management methodologies: spiral and waterfall development methods. We will discuss iterative and incremental design workflows and how to document the project progress. In the next chapter, we will apply this knowledge accompanied with Git functionalities in designing two use cases.

Workspace Template

The very first rule in maintaining a project is to avoid duplication. When two or more copies of the same document exist inside a project, there is a chance that these copies evolve differently overtime, and you end up with two different versions of the same file. This discrepancy is potentially harmful and could cause data loss. For example, suppose we join an electronic circuit design project that is also shared with another team. Within the project workspace, we create a text file, named updates.txt inside the documents folder, and record the design decisions inside it. At the same time, the other team decides to create updates.txt inside the notes folder without informing us with their decision. In this situation, we have two copies of updates.txt inside the workspace. This would cause confusion! Which of the files is the most updated? What should we do if their contents are not similar? To keep away from the "data inconsistency" problem, we need to apply procedures that avoid duplication inside the repository.

Note   The first rule in effective project management is to have one and only one copy of data inside the workspace. The data within files must be unique, and the files defined inside the workspace must be unique too.

A neat and well-organized workspace is the most effective tool for avoiding duplicates. Organizing documents in a structured manner and following the guidelines that are accepted by all team members reduces the chance of duplication and data loss. We propose the project structure shown in Figure 5-1. In the top level we have the company name, under which we have the project directory. So the next project is initiated under the company directory, but its inner structure is the same as the one shown in Figure 5-1.

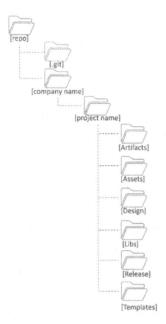

Figure 5-1. *The top-level organization of a circuit design project. Directories are designed such that each section of the project is stored in a separate folder*

The *Artifact* folder includes documents that were produced or collected during the project development. The inner structure of this folder is shown in Figure 5-2. Documents related to similar products such as catalog, brochure, and any other document related to available options provided by the other manufacturers are inserted in this folder. This is specifically important for selecting critical units, such as microcontroller, microprocessor units, FPGA chipsets, power manager IC, bus controller, and amplifiers. These units usually come with a wide range of documents that discuss different perspectives of the components.[1] Collecting the original documents that were provided by the manufacturers and storing

---

[1] You may look at the stm32U5 microcontroller series. On the product web page, you can find 50 application notes and technical manuals.

them inside the "Similar Products" directory could be useful in two ways: First, it shows the designer mindset over the project progress. Anytime the design team decides to evaluate an alternative in their design, they bring the documents within this folder and make a new commit into the local repository. Overtime, we can trace the history of all alternatives that were evaluated by the designers. The second benefit is that in this way we protect online documents against depreciation. After a while manufacturers deprecate their product and withdraw the resources from their web pages. This can be problematic for future designs.

Electronic components' datasheets are inserted in the namesake folder. Usually we need only collect the important datasheets; there is no need to store all datasheets. We store design guidelines such as PCB and EMC/EMI standards, design recommendations, white papers, and design rules in the "Design Guides" directory.

For special components, manufacturers provide development, evaluation, or test boards. These boards are useful for getting introduced to the components themselves. It is a good practice to store a copy of the documents related to the development boards in the "Development Boards" folder.

Errata files provided by component manufacturers are stored in the namesake folder. We need to emphasize that our own project's errata list is not stored in this folder.

Documents such as technical user manual, requirement document, technical guidelines, installation guidelines, handouts, and any other note that is made during the development (e.g., technical emails, meeting brief, stakeholder expectations list, etc.) are inserted inside the "Reports" folder.

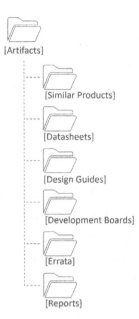

Figure 5-2. *Development documents, images, and notes are stored inside the Artifact folder. Each subsection is stored in a specific directory*

Within the *Assets* folder, the images and screenshots are stored. The images, artworks, and logos are stored inside "Images." These graphical elements are used for writing documents, reports, and schematics. Screenshots of the schematics, PCB, and manufacturing 3D model are used for presentations and short reports. These documents are stored in the "Screenshots" folder.

Besides this, we insert special third-party software in the *Assets* folder (Figure 5-3). Examples of such software tools are drivers, development board tools, programmer software, terminal tools, etc. We should only keep the legacy tools or those that are on the edge of depreciation by their vendors in this directory. Actively upgraded software such as compilers, development tools, and project management tools are not required to be copied inside this directory.

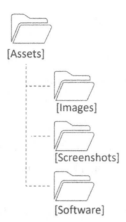

Figure 5-3. *Internal organization of the Assets directory*

Inside the Libs directory, the schematics libs, PCB libs, and integrated component libraries are inserted. The 3D models that are used in PCB libraries are stored in a separate folder (Figure 5-4).

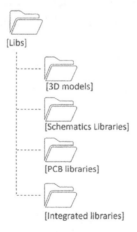

Figure 5-4. *PCB libraries, schematics, and integrated libraries are stored in separate folders in the Libs folder. 3D models that are used in the PCB library are kept inside the "3D models" directory*

After finishing with the design and development, the final outputs are inserted inside the *Release* folder (Figure 5-5). It includes all files that are required for manufacturers. The final 3D model of the completed circuit is stored in the "3D model" directory. Assembling documents such as housing details and its 3D model, PCB border graphics, and all sidenotes that are required for assembling the board are inserted in the 'Assembly" folder.

Software such as microcontroller firmware, FPGA synthesis output, developed programs and tools, operating system image, and so on that are needed to be loaded into the board in the manufacturing site are inserted in the "Firmware" folder.

PCB manufacturing materials such as GERBER files, drill files, stack layer files, and technical specifications of the production such as minimum and maximum drill sizes and minimum and maximum trace widths are inserted in the "PCB Manufacturing" folder.

For the sake of ease of sharing the project, it is a good practice to make a PDF from the schematics and insert it inside the "Schematics Diagrams" directory. This is very useful for sharing the design with nontechnical stakeholders who have no access to the PCB design software but are interested in reviewing the design.

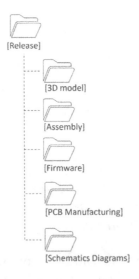

Figure 5-5. *Release documents are used for manufacturing*

Note   The contents of the *Release* folder are not allowed to change! You can think about this special directory as a one-way storage with only inward data flow, but it does not allow any manipulation or update. After inserting data into the *Release* folder, a new commit with a release number must be submitted. After preparing the next version, all the contents of the directory are cleared first, and then they are replaced with new version files and submitted again.

Besides the previous folders, we have a *Design* folder in the root level of the workspace. The design process happens inside this folder. Files such as schematics and PCB files are continuously updated inside this directory. The microcontroller firmware, FPGA synthesis, and configurations are all developed inside this directory. After finishing with development, the contents are relocated into their corresponding directories. The GERBER, manufacturing, assembling, schematic PDF, and firmware files are moved into the *Release* folder, errata files are inserted in the "Errata" folder, and so on. However, the latest version of the schematics (e.g., .sch, .SchDoc, etc.) and PCB files (.pcb, .PcbDoc, etc.) is kept in the *Design* folder. The *Design* folder is shared between all team members, and they actively contribute to it. So it is possible to have conflicts. For this reason, all team members are required to actively make commits into the local repository when they make a change in the contents of the *Design* folder.

Within the *Templates* directory, we keep document templates such as schematics template, progress report templates, requirements templates, risk list template, and any other template that is used in the project's reports.

Project Development Workflow

Circuit design and development projects should follow a systematic approach. Historically, for software applications, a variety of methodologies such as scrum, waterfall, Extreme Programming (XP), etc. are being applied. With considering the project's scale, proficiency of the team members, available tools, development environment, and budget, the project leader applies a methodology. On the other hand, circuit design projects are intrinsically different from software projects:

1. Circuit design projects are plain modular. A circuit is categorized into three sections: power supply, analog modules, and digital modules. Inside each of these sections, a set of transmitters, amplifiers, filters, input/output (IO), and processing units exist.

2. Circuit engineering projects are well-defined problems. Inputs, outputs, and the relation between them are clear in comparison with software projects.

3. Circuit designs are less subject to changes or updated requirements from the user. It is a rare occasion that new features must be added to a circuit. This contrasts with the software project in which new requirements and updates may be requested on a weekly basis.

So we can adapt a software development methodology for a circuit design project; however, due to the modularity, requirements' stability, and transparency of a circuit design project, we can apply simple methodologies such as waterfall or spiral development (Figure 5-6).

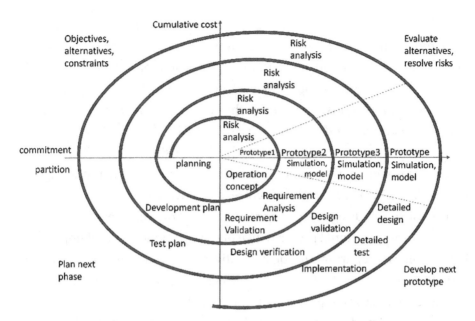

Figure 5-6. *Spiral development method: The project development lifetime repeatedly passes through four phases: planning, objective and alternative identification, evaluation, and development*

Spiral development is a risk-centric and prototype delivery methodology. It is usually good for complex projects. The project plan has two dimensions: the radial distance shows the cumulative cost, and the angular dimension represents the achieved progress for completing a circle.

The spiral development method has four separate phases: planning, objective and alternative identification, evaluation and assessment of the risks, and development and prototyping. The inner circle starts with a simplified planning. At the early stage this plan is very generic, and it does not include all the details. After preparing a road map, the next step is to find alternatives and available solutions. At this point, the options could be selection of a module in favor of another, or it could be a strategic decision such as outsourcing a section of the project. The alternatives and the constraints are analyzed for risks, and a prototype of the final project is prepared. In the next iterations, these steps are repeated, but at each step more details are included, and a more sophisticated prototype is prepared.

This methodology is applicable for circuit design; however, we need to consider three points: First, before the very last iteration, prototypes are not fully functional, and they are just a demo of the final project, which is well documented and organized. Only after finishing the last iteration we could implement the whole circuit. Second, the spiral methodology emphasizes alternatives and their corresponding methods, which is very critical for circuit design. Analyzing the market price, continuity of the products, and functional performance of the component are all important in electronics. Preparing a list of alternatives and their limitations helps on the project's output. Third, circuit design for special devices such as medical devices is required to minimize all kinds of risks. As already mentioned, spiral development is risk centric, and in all cycles the risks are evaluated for predicting potential weaknesses.

The waterfall methodology is almost the first method that is used for software project management. The steps are requirement identification, system analysis, system design, and implementation. In the analysis step, the key question is "What should be done?" and in the design phase the question is "How to do it?" For complex projects, the project is divided into subsections, and then the waterfall steps are repeated for all sections. A modified version of the waterfall method is shown in Figure 5-7. On the left side, deliverables are decomposed and implemented, and on the right side, the deliverables are evaluated and integrated with each other and construct a bigger reliable unit. This methodology is also very useful for circuit design projects as it is simple and easy to understand.

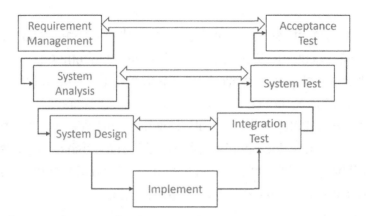

Figure 5-7. *Waterfall development model: In the V model, the left side corresponds to steps that end in a valuable output, and the right side is the evaluation and integration test that is applied on both the outputs of the level and the level beneath*

Documentation

Professionally developed projects are needed to be documented. For this, we can use template files that are prepared by experts. In this section we will review a few sample template files that are useful in both waterfall and spiral development.

Keeping track of the changes happening on the project documents is important such that whenever a team member makes an update to any of the project documents, they need to make a new commit and store the changes in the local Git repository.

Note   Documents are tools, but not the goal! They are prepared to clarify the customers' needs, formalize the requirements, and track the project progress overtime. The recent trend in software development is to reduce the burden of the documentation and instead concentrate on the outputs. However, this does not mean we do not require any document at all. To put it in a nutshell, there is a trade-off between documentation load and workload that calls for years of experience to get to the optimum point.

Iteration Plan

Despite all precautions, even experts' designs are not flawless. In the real world, it is common to build multiple prototypes before the final design. However, having an estimation of the required time and cost to prepare each prototype at the beginning of the project could help us have a better understanding about the project's progress. For this, we can use the "iteration plan" document. This document is prepared at the early stage of system design, but it is subject to updates overtime. A sample iteration plan is shown in Figure 5-8.

Revision History

Date	Version	Description	Author

Table of Contents

1.Objectives
2.Scope
3.References
4.Plan
     4.1   Iteration Activities
     4.2   Iteration Deliverables
5.Resources
     5.1   Staffing Resources
     5.2   Financial Resources
     5.3   Equipment & Facilities
           Resources
6.Evaluation Criteria

Figure 5-8. *Iteration plan document template: This document is prepared at the project's beginning, and it includes time and budget plans of the project*

The Objectives section introduces the domain of the document. For example, we can use the following:

This iteration plan describes the detailed plans for the iterations of the ... project. During each iteration, the requirements of the system will be (re-)defined, and the (high-level) plan for execution of the (sub-)project will be developed. This iteration document will conduct a thorough analysis on the system and will result in a decision on whether the project will proceed or not.

The Scope section identifies the boundaries of the iteration plan document:

> The iteration plan applies to the ... project being developed by ... This document will be used by the project manager and by the project team members.

Inside the Iteration Activities section, tasks that are related to the project iteration are listed (Table 5-1).

Table 5-1. *Example Iteration Activities table. Each activity for each iteration is written in a separate row. Each iteration could be written in a separate table*

Activity	Start Date	End date
Design PCB prototype 1	1 Jan 2021	13 Jan 2022
Manufacture prototype 1	14 Jan 2022	23 Jan 2022

In Iteration Deliverables, major outputs of each planned iteration are listed. These are the planned milestones that each iteration targets. In the Resources section, the assigned staff to the project, required equipment, and an estimate of the budget for each iteration are listed. At the end of the template, envisioned tests and evaluation criteria are provided.

This document is very useful for putting light on the project road. It provides a unique understanding between designers and customers. They will come to basic agreement about the project's future, timelines, and budget.

Risk Plan

Electrical projects are subject to two kinds of risks: environmental and technical. The environmental risks are divided into two subgroups: the first is organizational risks such as personnel and financial risks, and the other subgroup is infrastructure risks such as equipment-related risks. On the other hand, the technical risks are related to the project itself such as device safety, functionality, security, connectivity, and protection risks.

The project manager is required to make an early assessment about environmental risks and envision more accurate time and budget estimates. It is good practice to write down the risk list in a standard format (Figure 5-9) and continuously update it during the project progress.

Revision History

Date	Version	Description	Author

Table of Contents

1.Objectives
2.Scope
3.References
4.Risks
    4.1 <Risk Identifier>
      4.1.1 Risk Magnitude>
      4.1.2 Description
      4.1.3 Impact
      4.1.4 Indicators
      4.1.5 Mitigation Strategy
      4.1.6 Contingency Plan
    4.2 <Next Risk Identifier>

Figure 5-9. *Environmental risk list template: The team manager should envision a list of all potential events that could have a negative effect on the project progress. This list is essential for preparing alternatives*

In Figure 5-9, the first three sections are prepared like Figure 5-8. In section 4, a list of risks are provided. Each risk item has a unique identifier such as a unique code or a name. Each risk item is discussed from six points of view: a quantitative range (e.g., high, medium, low), a short description, the impact on the project, indicators that show when the risk happened, mitigation strategy to avoid the risk, and alternative plans for the case the risk happened.

From the engineering perspective, we need to have a precise understanding about the technical risks. These technical risks include a comprehensive evaluation from all project units such as the firmware, hardware design, manufacturing practices, and assembling issues. Even experienced engineers may design boards with an incorrect screw terminal or select a component with mismatching mechanical dimensions such that the soldering machine cannot place it on the board. These are risks that call for experiences; however, there are functional risks that have already been identified and standardized by authorities. For example, in "EN 61131-2 Programmable controllers – Equipment requirements and tests," the requirements and tests for Programmable Logic Controller (PLC) systems are discussed, and in "EN 61010-1 Safety requirements for electrical equipment for measurement, control, and laboratory use," the safety boundaries for general-purpose electrical equipment are standardized. These standards are a very promising source to identify the risks associated with the project. So consulting with the applicable standards is very useful before getting into the design of the circuit.

Version Control of an Electronic Project

Before finishing this chapter, we need to see how Git treats electrical circuit design projects. Git is sensitive to any changes happening inside the files, but in circuit design projects, we are not interested in recording all changes! For example, using KiCad EDA, we prepare an op-amp schematics (Figure 5-10) and submit the project into the local repository.

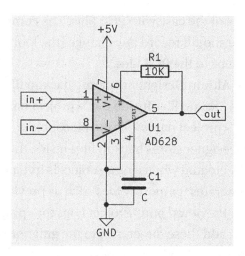

Figure 5-10. *Sample op-amp circuit prepared using KiCad. Any change such as changing the location of a component on the sheet could trigger Git with an update event*

Then without making any changes in the components or connections, we relocate the diagram on the sheet. In KiCad, schematics are text files. So, if we use the git diff command to compare the changes, we will see (snippet of the output is shown)

```
$ git diff --cached demo02.kicad_sch
- (wire (pts (xy 90.17 53.34) (xy 87.63 53.34))
+ (wire (pts (xy 105.41 64.77) (xy 102.87 64.77))
```

Usually, this level of details is not interesting to be stored as a separate Git commit.

Note   Separate commits for each update in the schematics sheets should be constructed when a component, a connection, or a sheet property is updated.

However, this is not the case with PCB files. The component location is important, and we should record any change (the footprint relocation included) that happens to the PCB files.

Both KiCad and Altium Designer generate backup files during project design. KiCad stores backup files inside the "<project name>-backup" folder in which the "<project name>" is the placeholder for the project name, and Altium Designer stores backup files inside the "History" folder that is automatically created when a new project is initiated. In addition, Altium Designer generates temporary files such as preview and log files that are stored in "__Previews" and "Project Logs for <project name>", respectively. We can add these directories to the gitignore list such that they do not participate in the remote repository.

Empirically, in electronic circuit projects, the main question is "Who designed? When was it designed?" To get the answer of these questions, we can use the log history with a formatted search query:

```
$ git log --all --graph --pretty=format:"%h %an %s"
```

Summary

In this chapter we reviewed a workspace structure for a circuit design project. The contents and their organization were discussed in detail. Then we discussed the importance of a systematic approach in project management. Specifically, we reviewed the importance of the iteration and risk plan documents, and we provided templates for each of them. We discussed a few points about the application of Git in circuit design projects. In the next chapter, we will apply the content of this chapter for developing circuit projects.

CHAPTER 6

Application

In this chapter we use Git in developing two open source circuit design projects. We will see how Git is a functional tool for managing projects. In this chapter we will try to study how to develop a project using systematic approaches discussed in Chapter 5 and how Git's tools can be useful in each step.

The first project is SyncBox. It is an open source modular system that is aimed to unify the radiology scanners. In this project we will review how Altium Designer supports Git, how to manage a project in GitHub, how to get feedback, and how to implement an issue tracking system. The second project is a Raspberry Pi (RPi) Computer Module 4 IO board. In this project we will find how Git could help us make a collaboration environment between team members, share projects between team members, and resolve conflicts and learn the importance of the meaningful commit messages – all in KiCad.

Case Study: SyncBox

An X-ray scanner is made of four different main units: i) a high-voltage power source, ii) an X-ray tube that turns the power into X-ray beam, iii) X-ray scanner that converts X-ray to an image, and iv) a workstation computer that communicates with devices, captures detector images, and processes them. The connection diagram of the device is shown in Figure 6-1. In this diagram, the data and control lines are shown in green, and the power line is in red.

© Altay Brusan and Aytac Durmaz 2022
A. Brusan and A. Durmaz, *Git for Electronic Circuit Design*, Maker Innovations Series,
https://doi.org/10.1007/978-1-4842-8124-6_6

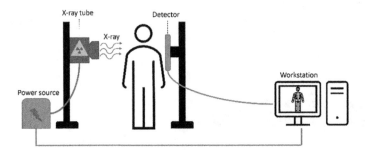

Figure 6-1. *X-ray scanner. It has four main units: power source, X-ray tube, detector, and workstation computer. The green lines are data/ control cables, and the red line is the power line*

For each patient, the radiology technician registers a request on the workstation at first. Then, the workstation informs the power source with the new request. When the power source is ready, it informs the workstation with a ready signal. After receiving this signal, the workstation asks for the technician's confirmation, and it sends the start signal back to the power source. At the same time, the workstation informs the detector to start capturing a new image. After the shooting is finished, the workstation fetches the captured (raw) image from the detector into itself and starts processing it.

The issue with modern radiology scanners is that there is no specific standard for communicating with components. Each vendor power source and detector has its own set of communication API and timing signals, which are not always compatible with the other vendors. Additionally, the physical communication channel between the workstation and peripherals is not standardized. Some vendors are in favor of legacy serial protocols such as RS-232, while the others prefer modern protocols such as USB and wireless channels.

SyncBox is an open source hardware platform that is designed as an umbrella over the heterogeneous ecosystem of radiology manufacturers. It provides a vast range of interfaces for almost all available X-ray units (Figure 6-2). Additionally, its general-purpose input/output (GPIO) lines provide an extension bus for future applications. The only requirement to integrate a new component into SyncBox is to add its driver into the SyncBox firmware. To put it in a nutshell, SyncBox is a device that lets us make our own radiology scanner with minimum effort. It lets us democratize the medical radiology systems.

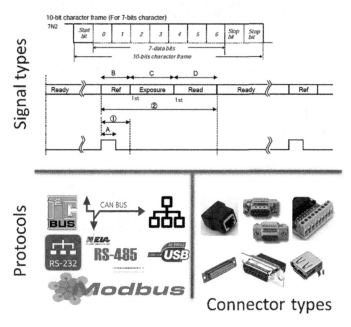

Figure 6-2. *The communication signals, protocol, and connector type of each unit are different from device to device*

We will review the SyncBox design and development over the waterfall methodology. Step by step, we trace the application of Git and GitHub for managing the project.

Step 1: Requirement Analysis

In waterfall workflow, the first step is to identify the requirements. These requirements should be collected inside the requirement analysis document. A template of such a document is shown in Figure 6-3.

It is important to note that requirements are divided into five different categories: Functionality, Usability, Reliability, Performance, and Supportability (FURPS).

Revision History

Date	Version	Description	Author

Table of Contents

1. Introduction
   1.1 Purpose
   1.2 Scope
   1.3 Definitions, Acronyms and Abbreviations
   1.4 References
   1.5 Overview

2. Functionality
   2.1 <Functional Requirement One>

3. Usability
   3.1 <Usability Requirement One>

4. Reliability
   4.1 <Reliability Requirement One>

5. Performance
   5.1 <Performance Requirement One>

6. Supportability
   6.1 <Supportability Requirement One>

7. Design Constraints
   7.1 <Design Constraint One>

8. Online User Documentation and Help System Requirements

9. Purchased Components

10. Interfaces
    10.1 User Interfaces
    10.2 Hardware Interfaces
    10.3 Software Interfaces
    10.4 Communications Interfaces

11. Licensing Requirements

12. Legal, Copyright and Other Notices

13. Applicable Standards

Figure 6-3. *Template used to collect the system requirements. The requirements include five different categories: Functionality, Usability, Reliability, Performance, and Supportability (FURPS)*

In the first section, the general scope of the document, definitions, abbreviations, and references are written. This section in the document is supposed to be concise such that the reader will get quick information over what they are about to read.

The *Functionality* requirements include all our expectations from the device: what the system is supposed to do. In the case of SyncBox

- Provide a communication channel for the detector.

- Provide a communication channel for the power source.

- Provide a high-speed data channel to transfer data from the detector.

- Provide an emergency stop.

- Provide a voice alarm during X-ray exposure.

- Provide a platform for executing radiology applications.

The next requirement aspect is *Usability*. In a single world, SyncBox should be easy to use with no a priori knowledge. It should be designed such that if an existing workstation is replaced by SyncBox, there would be no need for training the users. It is supposed to provide three interfaces: a power button, a reset button, and an optional touch screen for special applications.

The *Reliability* of the device should be estimated in quantitative methods. The common criteria are

- Mean time between failures (MTBF): 6 months

- Availability: 99% of the time

- Mean time to repair (MTTR): 24 hours

- Accuracy: 1 ms in producing timing signals

- Maximum bugs: Two bugs/function

- Bug rate: Minor and warnings

There are different approaches to estimate a device's *Performance*. The common approaches are the performance of the most critical functionality, the average performance on all functionalities, and the maximum required performance among all functionalities. In the case of SyncBox, reacting to the emergency situations is the most critical and demands for maximum performance. The criteria for this situation are as follows:

- Response time for a transaction: 10 ms

- Throughput: 100 transactions per second

- Capacity: One sound alarm, one emergency stop button, and one mechanical intervention channel

- Degradation mode: At least 98% stability

- Resource utilization: Alarm circuit

In the *Supportability* section, the conventions and utilities that are used to maintain or enhance the system support are listed. For SyncBox we have the following:

- The project is developed in Altium Designer 20. The project files are valid till the end of the version's life.

- The source files are maintained on GitHub.

- Issue tracking and community feedback management systems are based on the GitHub platform.

In *Design Constraints* the physical dimension and the utilities used in developing the SyncBox firmware are mentioned. Also, SyncBox is required to execute a workstation software tool, so a processor is needed. The processor should be supported by off-the-shelf operating systems such as Microsoft Windows and Linux. The *online documentation* is not mandatory, but the design documentations are required to be shared through a GitHub repository. The *purchased components* are bill of materials (BOM) used in the circuit, development boards, operating system license, and Altium Designer license. SyncBox has a simple interaction interface. In this regard, a power button and a reset button are the mandatory physical interfaces, but it could be augmented by an optional touch screen interface.

SyncBox is an open source project distributed under LGPL; however, it is not a medical product, and the users are required to apply for the certificate by themselves. For commercial applications, it is required to be compatible with the medical standards such as IEC 606001-2-8 Particular requirements for safety; IEC 61010-2 Safety requirements for electrical equipment for measurement, control, and laboratory use; IEC 61131-2 Equipment requirements and tests; ACR–AAPM–SIIM–SPR practice parameter for digital radiography; ACR–AAPM–SIIM technical standard for electronic practice; and ACR–AAPM–SIIM technical standard of medical imaging.

Step 2: System Analysis

After engineering the requirements, the next step is to analyze the system. In this step we prepare iteration plan and risk assessment documents. These documents accompanied with the requirement analysis help us keep on a continuous path and avoid diverging overtime, which is a common trap the novice engineers fall in.

Figuring out the risks and assessing their potential harm is a complex process and demands for experience. However, as a rule of thumb, we can identify risks (or at least important ones) by looking at the requirement document and asking the questions "How can it go wrong?" and " What would be the consequences?" for each requirement. For SyncBox this includes:

- Risk identifier: GPIO_PROTECT.

- Description: The GPIO pins are not standard. The voltage levels and logic (inverse or direct) are different for different circuits. There is a need for a protection circuit for all different combinations.

- Risk magnitude: High.

- Impact: Could cause permanent or serious damages to the circuit.

- Indicator: SyncBox does not react to the GPIO channel.

- Mitigation strategy: Design a general-purpose protection circuit.

- Contingency plan: Use a standard communication bus.

For the next risk

- Risk identifier: PWR_PROTECT.

- Description: The input power is provided by an external 12 V 4 A AC/DC adaptor. The input power could exceed this limit.

- Risk magnitude: High.

- Impact: Could cause permanent or serious damages to the circuit.

- Indicator: Magic smoke!

- Mitigation strategy: By designing a protection circuit in the input, such that the input ranges should be explicitly written on the plug.

- Contingency plan: Replace the complete circuit or protection unit.

The risks are not limited to the device functionality alone. Human factors are also important in identifying risks:

- Risk identifier: INACCUR_FOOTPRN.

- Description: Processing units such as FPGA, CPU, GPU, or power management ICs may have no self-descriptive footprint or description.

- Risk magnitude: Low.

- Impact: The PCB burnout and magic smoke!

- Indicator: Circuits burn out.

- Mitigation strategy: For all processing chipsets, the footprint should be controlled and confirmed. This includes studying the similar product that applied that component in their design or asking the manufacturer for extra information.

- Contingency plan: Replace the circuit.

The environmental risks are also important, for example:

- Risk identifier: TEMP_LIMT.

- Description: The environment temperature may exceed the system range.

- Risk magnitude: Medium.

- Impact: Could cause the data to be lost.

- Indicator: System resets or behave with reduced performance.

- Mitigation strategy: Select components that work in the range of the target environment (radiology room) and consider a cooling fan in the system design.

- Contingency plan: Cool down the environment.

Some risks are defined in standards, for example:

- Risk identifier: EMC_LIMIT.

- Description: SyncBox should be able to pass the EN-55011 EMC test requirements.

- Risk magnitude: High.

211

- Impact: Not suitable to be introduced to the market.

- Indicator: The certified body will reject the device.

- Mitigation strategy: Apply multilayer PCB with ground plate, component positioning should follow the best practices, apply decoupling capacitors, and match the impedance of the traces with the standards.

- Contingency plan: Redesign the circuit.

We need to emphasize that this version of the risk analysis document is not complete. Overtime, by the project progress, we'll find out more details, and we'll need to revisit the risk document; however, writing the risks at the beginning of the project could inform all team members with the limitations. In this way all the team members could have the same understanding of the project.

Step 3: System Design

The next document we need to design is iteration planning. This document is useful for identifying the major milestones. To find out the milestones, we need to answer two questions: "What is a *valuable* achievement?" and "When is it going to be ready?" Answering these questions requires making some *design decisions*! For example, SyncBox needs a CPU and a microcontroller to run its tasks. The CPU is responsible for computationally intensive operations, while the microcontroller is responsible for device-level synchronization tasks. The architecture and implementation details are not specified in the requirement document. In the iteration plan these architectural designs should be settled down because they directly affect the deliverables and timelines of the project. In the case of SyncBox, we can use an off-the-shelf Computer on Module (CoM) card and design an extension card with a microcontroller, or we can implement both CPU and microcontroller circuits in one card from scratch, or we may simulate the microcontroller using a CPU (Figure 6-4).

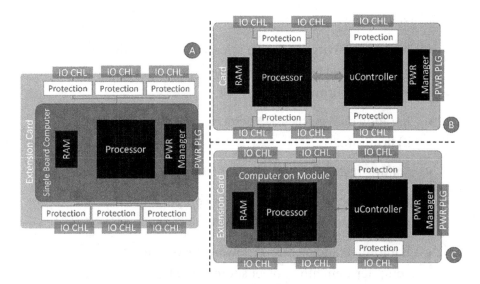

Figure 6-4. *Three different methods to implement SyncBox: A)
Use a single-board computer such as BeagleBone Black and design
an extension card with protected IO channels. B) Implement both
processor and microcontroller on a single board. C) Computer on
Module (CoM) is an off-the-shelf component mounted on the top of a
newly designed extension card*

The decisions that are made in this step could change the whole
product. We need to emphasize that the chain of decisions should be made
based on the trade-off between cost, time, and availability. While a chain
of correct decisions could boost up the project and increase the success
rate, the wrong decisions could end up in failure.

For SyncBox, an extension card with an off-the-shelf Computer on
Module (CoM) architecture is preferred. In this way all high-frequency and
complex units such as CPU-RAM bus, graphic interfaces, and high-speed
terminals are available on a single board. This approach increases the
development speed. On the extension card there is a microcontroller that
is responsible to communicate with low-speed serial devices or requires
accurate timing signals.

The first iteration plan is

- Iteration activity: i) Select a microcontroller, ii) design and develop a board for the microcontroller, iii) and implement firmware.

- Iteration deliverables: i) Microcontroller (proof) board, ii) firmware.

- Staffing resources: Two electronics engineers.

- Financial resource: 6000 USD for components, in addition to payments and invoices.

- Equipment and facility: Firmware development compiler, benchtop power source, oscilloscope, bill of materials used in circuit design.

The second iteration plan is

- Iteration activity: i) Select Computer on Module, ii) design and develop a board for the selected board, iii) and integrate the board with the first iteration board.

- Iteration deliverables: An extension card for a CoM board.

- Staffing resources: Two electronics engineers and one software developer.

- Financial resource: 10000 USD for components, in addition to payments and invoices.

- Equipment and facility: Firmware development compiler, benchtop power source, oscilloscope, spectrum analyzer, bill of materials used in circuit design.

The third iteration plan is

- Iteration activity: Design the complete board.

- Iteration deliverables: A completed release of SyncBox.

- Staffing resources: Three electronics engineers, two software engineers, and a mechanical designer.

- Financial resource: 15000 USD for components, in addition to payments and invoices.

- Equipment and facility: Laboratory benchtop power source, oscilloscope, spectrum analyzer, bill of materials used in circuit design.

The timeline of the iterations is as follows (Table 6-1).

Table 6-1. *Activity timeline for each iteration*

Activity	Start Date	End date
Design and implement microcontroller board	13 Jun 2021	12 Jul 2021
Design and implement CoM extension card	14 Jul 2021	24 Sep 2021
Design and implement complete board	26 Sep 2021	28 Dec 2021

There are few points within this planning document. First, in each iteration the deliverables are extended. The first iteration focuses on the microcontroller circuit, in the second iteration this circuit is extended to the CPU circuit, and in the third iteration the complete circuit is delivered. Also, the first iteration output is a dev board (proof board) circuit, and there is no need for a finished PCB. This will reduce the development time and let the firmware developers start their tasks immediately without a need for a completed prototype (if the selected microcontroller has a dev board, we can use it as the platform for developing firmware).

The iterations' deliverables must be functional and stay within the acceptance range defined in the requirements. For nontrivial projects this is not achievable without a few trial and error. So, within each iteration, we may need to print PCB boards multiple times. It is a good practice to annotate boards with the iteration number and the number of the trial.

Step 4: Implementation

After preparing the documents, we are ready to initiate the project. The first step is to create the project structure inside the Git repository as discussed in Chapter 5 (Figure 6-5). Then we add risk analysis, iteration management, and requirement management documents one by one to the *Artifacts* ➤ *Reports* directory and commit them individually into the local repository.

Figure 6-5. *The internal structure of the project*

The firmware developers can start their development on a dev board before the circuit designers' contribution comes out. In that case, we can create an independent branch for them, such that on the master (main) branch the circuit designers commit their contributions and on feat/ firmware software developers insert their commits. At the end of iterations, these branches join with each other. This will help us minimize the risk of conflicts between the two groups:

```
$ git log --oneline
a23c7e5 (HEAD -> master) project iteration plan document added
427f673 project risk list document added
4b8ff3e requirements specification document added
f64bc88 initialize the empty project directory structure
```

We can add a gitignore file inside the "Design" folder that targets Altium Designer temporary files:

```
$ git log --oneline
e6c01fc (HEAD -> master) gitignore is created in Design directory
a23c7e5 (origin/master) project iteration plan document added
427f673 project risk list document added
4b8ff3e requirements specification document added
f64bc88 initialize the empty project directory structure
```

Now the circuit design engineers start the first iteration. In this iteration the focus is on the microcontroller. Among the available options, by considering price, availability in the local market, technical support, and product longevity, the PIC24 microcontroller is selected. To make this conclusion, a thorough investigation is accomplished by studying the guidelines and other materials provided by the manufacturers. These documents are inserted into the *Artifacts* ➤ *Design Guides* directory and then committed into the repository:

```
$ git log --oneline
9b3cd4c (HEAD -> master, origin/master) PIC design guide files
included
8b4dd63 new development board added
e6c01fc gitignore is created in Design directory
a23c7e5 project iteration plan document added
427f673 project risk list document added
4b8ff3e requirements specification document added
f64bc88 initialize the empty project directory structure
```

> **Note**   Sharing technical documents through a Git repository and regular discussion about them help the team members have a glance over each other's thought direction. This is very useful for knowledge circulation among the team members and increases the cooperation spirit.

While the circuit designers do their study, the firmware developers start to develop the firmware based on the available dev board. They insert their contributions in the feat/firmware branch:

```
MINGW64  (FEAT/firmware)
$ git log --oneline --graph
* 2411ca0 (HEAD -> FEAT/firmware, origin/FEAT/firmware)
firmware project config updated
* 53f4cf3 touch screen firmware created
* 2cc8ef8 project documentations created
* ba7ca65 bootloader is added to firmware
* c9fd125 firmware project initialized
* 9b3cd4c (origin/master, master) PIC design guide files included
* 8b4dd63 new development board added
* e6c01fc gitignore is created in Design directory
* a23c7e5 project iteration plan document added
* 427f673 project risk list document added
* 4b8ff3e requirements specification document added
* f64bc88 initialize the empty project directory structure
```

> **Note**   It is not a good idea to create a separate branch for each developer/designer. The best practice is to create a branch for each new feature, bug, or independent subsystem. When the objective of the branch is finished, it is joined with the master (main) branch.

Remember, creating a separate branch for each contributor only postpones the conflicts to sometime later and it increases the chance of a complete chaos. So avoid branch-based separation and try to integrate the contributions on a daily basis.

After circuit designers finish with the proof board (Figure 6-6), they should prepare a technical report that includes details such as the assumption that they made in their design (e.g., analog input pins are all grounded), circuit specifications (e.g., IO port order on the board), and future improvement notes. The technical manuscript is usually confidential, and there is no specific template for that; however, it should clearly be mentioned in which iteration the document is prepared or updated. This document is stored in the *Artifacts* ➤ *Reports* directory and committed to the local repository when it is updated.

Figure 6-6. *SyncBox dev board. After constructing the board, it should be supported by a technical manuscript that includes assumptions, specifications, and future improvements*

At this point the first iteration is finished, and we can merge feat/
firmware on master. This is the commit we can tag with "version 1":

```
$ git tag -am "end of Iteration 1" V1.0
$ git log --oneline --all --graph
*   bc7b3f3 (HEAD -> master, tag: V1.0) Merge branch 'feat/
    firmware'
|\
| * 2411ca0 (origin/FEAT/firmware, FEAT/firmware) firmware
project config updated
| * 53f4cf3 touch screen firmware created
| * 2cc8ef8 project documentations created
| * ba7ca65 bootloader is added to firmware
| * c9fd125 firmware project initialized
* | 8b0f2a3 (origin/master) SyncBox prototype reports added
|/
* 9b3cd4c PIC design guide files included
* 8b4dd63 new development board added
* e6c01fc gitignore is created in Design directory
* a23c7e5 project iteration plan document added
* 427f673 project risk list document added
* 4b8ff3e requirements specification document added
* f64bc88 initialize the empty project directory structure
```

Now the circuit design team starts the second iteration. At first, a
complete study over all available Computer on Module (CoM) options
is accomplished, and the best option that meets the SyncBox processing
requirements is selected. Artifacts and materials that are used in the
comparative study should be stored in their corresponding sub-folders
within *Artifact*:

```
$ git log --oneline
5f8530b (HEAD -> master) kontron and connect tech
documents added
bc7b3f3 (tag: V1.0) Merge branch 'feat/firmware'
...
```

After making a decision on the CoM module, the circuit engineers start designing. Schematics and PCB design files are created inside the *Design* directory. To minimize the conflicts between commits that come from different engineers, each designer is assigned to a set of schematics and is not allowed to touch on the other sheets (Figure 6-7). The complete template of SyncBox is available in the Git repository. It is worth to mention Altium has built-in multi-channel and multi-sheet tools that help graphically separate the sheets between team members.

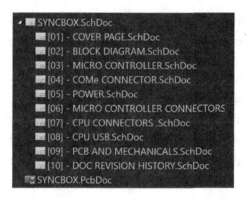

Figure 6-7. *Multi-sheet template. Each designer is responsible for a specific set of sheets and is not allowed to make a change on the others*

In the simple case, each designer is responsible for designing an independent subset of schematics. As they are working on separate sheets, the chance of conflicts between commits is reduced. The input/output ports define the connection lines between sheets, and their names are required to be a priori known between all team members. For this reason, it is a good practice to have a naming convention rule, which is accepted by all members.

221

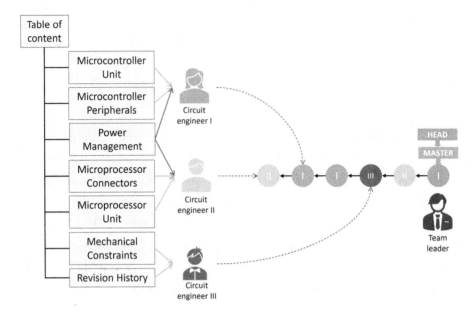

Figure 6-8. *Simplified schematic diagram for SyncBox. Each contributor is responsible for a section within the diagram*

In realistic scenarios some schematics are required to be designed by multiple designers at the same time. For example, in Figure 6-8 two designers are responsible for preparing the power management unit. In these situations, each designer can create a temporary branch on the local repository and insert commits on the temporary branch. At the end, all temporary branches that are created for designing a specific sheet are merged. We should consider that these branches are temporary, so the number of commits within them should be limited and all the commits are around a specific sheet. In other words, designers are not allowed to manipulate anything else except a common schematic sheet, while they are switched on the temporary branch. In the case that the number of contributors is limited, we can use stash instead of creating a new branch.

Note   Temporary branches are useful for reducing the chance of conflicts during the design. Each user has their own branch. These branches include a limited number of commits, which are related to changes to one and only one sheet (the sheet that needs to be designed by multiple engineers).

Git is useful for team managers. They can use the log history as a very efficient tool to track the project progress. They also can analyze the information in the log history such as the date, time, and contributor to monitor the project progress, detect the bottleneck, and predict the project latencies. With monitoring log history, managers can evaluate the performance of each engineer. In some organizations the "number of commits per day" is accepted as a performance criterion. Despite the controversy about the efficiency of this criterion, it still provides an estimate for the relative performance of each team member and helps them avoid psychologically falling in the trap of self-sacrifice!

Step 5: Release

At the end of each iteration, a new version is ready. The manufacturing files such as bill of materials (BOM), firmware, GERBER files, schematic diagrams (if they are not confidential) in PDF format, and manufacturing files are required to be inserted inside the *Release* folder and committed into the repository. This commit can be tagged by a [iteration].[version] number. For example, in iteration 3 we are printing the board for the second time. We can tag the release as V3.2. The final release of Git is shown in Figure 6-9.

Figure 6-9. *SyncBox circuit release V3.0*

Altium Designer and Git

So far we have used the git bash environment for interacting with Git. If an Altium Designer project is created inside a Git workspace, we can use the Altium tools (Figure 6-10).

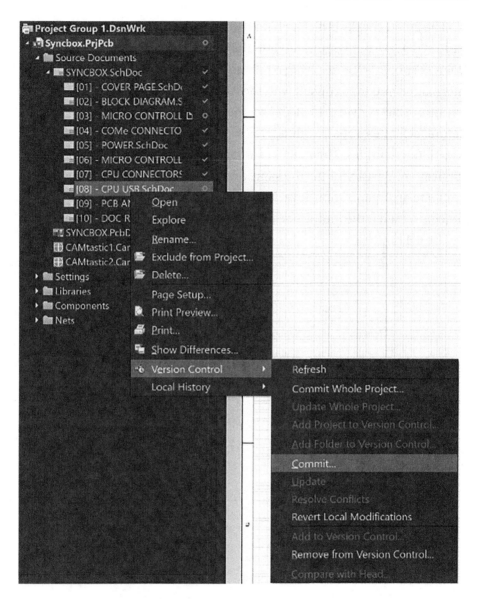

Figure 6-10. *Altium Designer supports Git. It supports comparison, commits, and conflict resolution*

The green checks indicate that the files are updated, and the red circles are files that are not committed into the repository yet. The Altium Git tool is very handy for resolving conflicts and comparing files. For more information you may consult with the Altium help tool.

Altium 365 provides PCB and schematics library sharing. This feature facilitates a central library bank architecture that is accessible from different nodes. The main advantage of library sharing is avoiding duplication. We can mimic the same architecture using Git. For this, we create an organization-level library repository (LibRepo), and in the projects we fetch the footprints and schematics stored inside LibRepo (Figure 6-11).

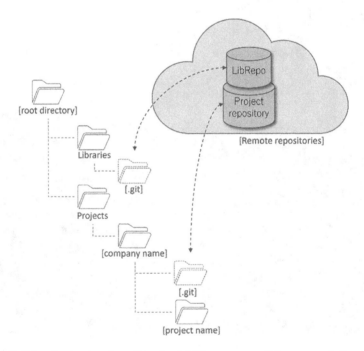

Figure 6-11. *An organization-level library repository architecture. LibRepo includes all schematics and PCB footprints. In any project the items stored inside this repository are recalled and updated*

Note   In the central library repository architecture, we should take special care for the access levels. It is a good practice to limit the add, remove, and update privileges to an administrator while all team members can read from (pull) the repository. These updates should be made in the central repository only after the administrator approved the incoming footprints.

It is worth to emphasize the Altium Git tool is not very versatile. To manage the branches, resolve conflicts, and solve maintenance problems, we need to directly consult with Git!

Case Study: RPi COM 4 Extension Board

In this project we need to develop a customized extension board for RPi COM 4. The original extension board comes with GPIO pins and configuration headers that we do not need in our application. For our requirements we need an extension board that supports one HDMI, two USBs, and a MicroSD socket.

The project source is prepared in KiCad EDA. This tool is freeware, which makes it a great option for open source projects; however, it does not support Git. In this section we will customize this board and focus on adopting strategies for comparing files, resolving conflicts, and implementing issue tracking systems.

Suppose we removed the following unit (Figure 6-12) from the GPIO schematics.

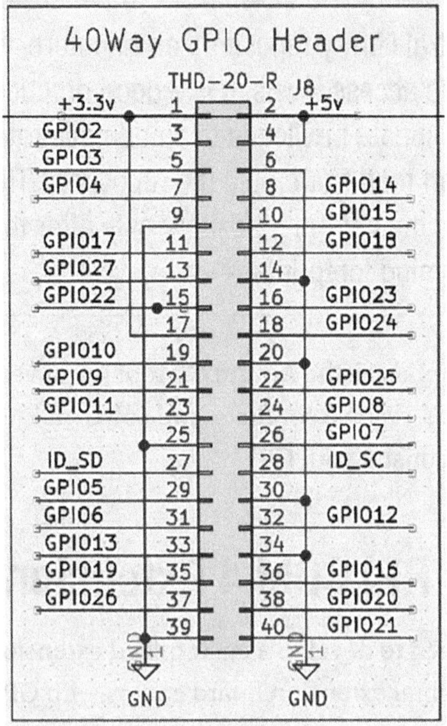

Figure 6-12. *40-way GPIO header we need to remove from the board*

The output of the diff command is (snippet is shown)

```
$ git diff --staged
diff --git a/Design/CM4IOv5.kicad_sch b/Design/CM4IOv5.
kicad_sch
index ee10fb9..30e11aa 100644
--- a/Design/CM4IOv5.kicad_sch
+++ b/Design/CM4IOv5.kicad_sch
@@ -954,12 +954,6 @@
     (path "/00000000-0000-0000-0000-00005cff706a/00000000-
     0000-0000-0000-00005dcc8bbc"
```

```
      (reference "#PWR0101") (unit 1) (value "GND")
      (footprint "")
    )
-   (path "/00000000-0000-0000-0000-00005cff706a/00000000-
    0000-0000-0000-00005ddd76da"
-     (reference "#PWR0102") (unit 1) (value "GND")
      (footprint "")
-   )
-   (path "/00000000-0000-0000-0000-00005cff706a/00000000-
    0000-0000-0000-00005ddf038e"
-     (reference "#PWR0103") (unit 1) (value "GND")
      (footprint "")
-   )
    (path "/00000000-0000-0000-0000-00005cff706a/00000000-
    0000-0000-0000-00005e15bd87"
      (reference "#PWR0104") (unit 1) (value "GND")
      (footprint "")
    )
```

The KiCad schematics are text files internally (despite Altium Designer). All connections and components are in text format. So the diff command treats the schematics as a text file and shows the result accordingly. However, most of the time this textual representation of a circuit is not self-clear enough. To compare the differences graphically, we can use stash:

```
$ git stash
Saved working directory and index state WIP on master: d7914d8
project loaded first time
```

Now if we reopen the schematics page, we would have what is shown in Figure 6-13.

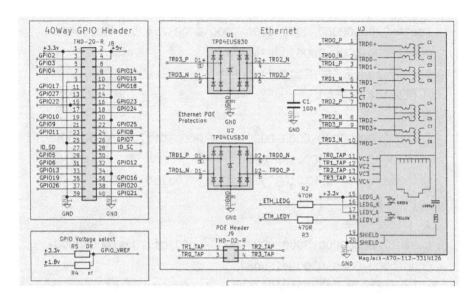

Figure 6-13. *After inserting the content of the workspace and index area content inside stash, the removed 40-way GPIO header returns*

Suppose another colleague is also working on the GPIO schematics. When we try to pull their contributions from the remote repository, we face conflicts:

```
$ git pull origin
Auto-merging Design/CM4_GPIO.kicad_sch
CONFLICT (content): Merge conflict in Design/CM4_GPIO.kicad_sch
Automatic merge failed; fix conflicts and then commit
the result.

MINGW64  (master|MERGING)
$ git status
On branch master
Your branch and 'origin/master' have diverged,
```

and have 1 and 1 different commits each, respectively.
  (use "git pull" to merge the remote branch into yours)

You have unmerged paths.
  (fix conflicts and run "git commit")
  (use "git merge --abort" to abort the merge)

Changes to be committed:
        modified: Design/CM4IOv5.kicad_sch

Unmerged paths:
  (use "git add <file>..." to mark resolution)
        both modified: Design/CM4_GPIO.kicad_sch

If we try to resolve the conflicts using Git's mergetool, then we may face something as shown in Figure 6-14. Trying to understand and resolve the conflict among thousands of lines is not easy at all.

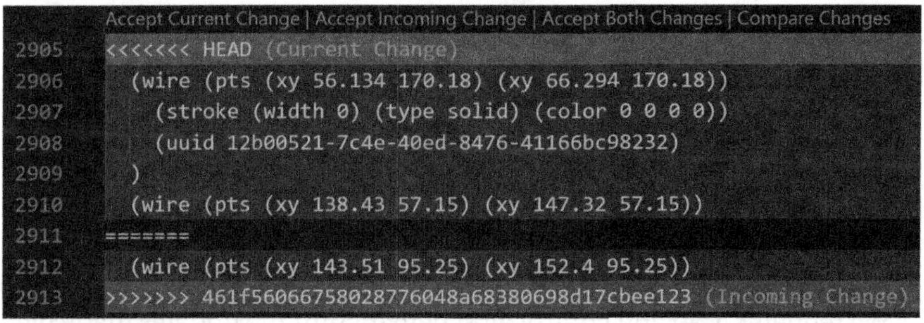

Figure 6-14. *mergetool for resolving conflicts in schematics is not very helpful*

In practice we can solve the conflict more easily. First, instead of pulling from the remote repository, we can use fetch as follows:

```
$ git fetch origin
remote: Enumerating objects: 9, done.
remote: Counting objects: 100% (9/9), done.
```

```
remote: Compressing objects: 100% (1/1), done.
remote: Total 5 (delta 4), reused 5 (delta 4), pack-reused 0
Unpacking objects: 100% (5/5), 736 bytes | 49.00 KiB/s, done.
From https://github.com/GitForEng/rpiext
   889bef3..461f560  master      -> origin/master
```

Then check the log history:

```
$ git log --oneline --all
0de286e (HEAD -> master) GPIO voltage select changed
461f560 (origin/master) J2 header removed from schematics
889bef3 40-way header removed
```

We check out the origin/master commit:

```
$ git checkout origin/master
Note: switching to 'origin/master'.
You are in 'detached HEAD' state. You can look around, make
experimental changes and commit them, and you can discard any
commits you make in this state without impacting any branches
by switching back to a branch.
HEAD is now at 461f560 J2 header removed from schematics
MINGW64  ((461f560...))
$
```

We reopen KiCad and control all schematics for the updates made by the other contributors, then return to our latest commit, and apply them on our schematics:

```
$ git checkout master
Previous HEAD position was 461f560 J2 header removed from
schematics
Switched to branch 'master'
Your branch and 'origin/master' have diverged,
```

and have 1 and 1 different commits each, respectively.
   (use "git pull" to merge the remote branch into yours)

If it is needed, we can reapply the same steps a couple of times till we make sure nothing is forgotten. After finishing with updating the latest commit, we try to pull from the remote repository. If we face any conflicts, we can be sure there was no serious issue (e.g., a component location on a sheet is changed). In this situation, we can use mergetool with the "accept the current changes" option:

```
 MINGW64  (master|MERGING)
$ git mergetool
No files need merging
```

```
MINGW64  (master|MERGING)
$ git merge --continue
[master ceac1aa] Merge branch 'master' of https://github.com/
GitForEng/rpiext
```

GitHub has excellent tools for tracking issues and managing projects. Inside the repository there is an "Issues" tab used for creating feedback for the project manager (Figure 6-15). An issue is any feedback related to the project such as a bug report, a question, or a new feature request. This tool is very handy compared to the old mailing lists or web log discussions.

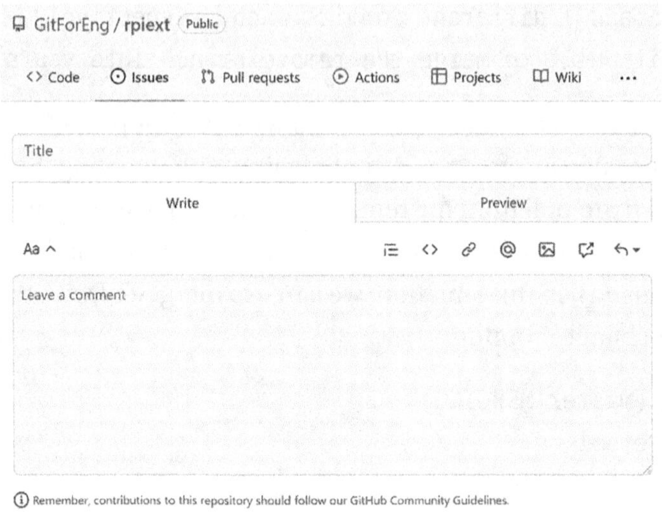

Figure 6-15. *GitHub issue tracking system*

Summary

In this chapter we reviewed the application of Git in circuit design projects. Step by step, we developed a circuit design project using the waterfall methodology. We studied how Git could be useful for observing the project progress and how to make more efficient commits. We saw that Altium Designer supports Git, which could potentially ease our job in resolving conflicts and comparing changes; however, this does not eliminate our need to know about Git completely. On the other hand, KiCad is not integrated with Git yet, and we need to do most of the jobs manually.

Correction to: Git for Electronic Circuit Design

Correction to:

Altay Brusan and Aytac Durmaz, *Git for Electronic Circuit Design*
https://doi.org/10.1007/978-1-4842-8124-6

This book was published without Series ID, Print ISSN number & Electronic ISSN Number. This has now been updated in the book with the Series ID - 17311, Print ISSN: 2948-2542 & Electronic ISSN: 2948-2550.

The updated version of this book can be found at
https://doi.org/10.1007/978-1-4842-8124-6

Index

A

add command, 44
--amend parameter, 170
Artifact folder, 186

B

Bill of materials (BOM), 208
Branches
    cancel merge, 109, 110
    change active branch, 67–71
    change name, 72
    cherry-pick, 107, 108
    commands, 118
    compare, 74, 75
    conflict files, 91–93, 95, 96
    creating, 66
    definition, 63
    delete, 72, 73
    FEATURE/A, 64
    HEAD, 65
    mergetool
        definition, 80
        FF, 80–83
        three-way merge, 84–91
    move on branch, 78, 79
    pointers, 63
    rebasing, 100–106
    reverted commit, 112–115
    squash merge, 96, 97, 99, 100
    stash, 76, 77
    tags, 117, 118

C

Central repository storage
    service, 121
checkout command, 57
Chunks, 36
Circuit design project
    development workflow, 192, 193
    documentation
        definition, 195
        iteration plan, 196–198
        risks plan, 199, 200
    electronic project, version
        control, 200, 202
    Git, 184, 202
    workflow, 183
    workspace template, 184–191
Commits
    change order, 178, 179
    combine, 180, 181
    definition, 165

© Altay Brusan and Aytac Durmaz 2022
A. Brusan and A. Durmaz, *Git for Electronic Circuit Design*, Maker Innovations Series,
https://doi.org/10.1007/978-1-4842-8124-6

Commits (*cont.*)
   garbage collection, 168, 169
   last, 170, 172
   middle, amend, 173–176
   published, 165, 166
   reflog command, 166, 167
   rewording commit message, 177
Computer-Aided Design (CAD), 1
Computer on Module (CoM), 212,
      213, 220
--continue parameter, 93

D

diff command, 228

E

Extreme Programming (XP), 192

F

Fast-forward (FF) merge, 80
Fork, 159
Functionality, Usability, Reliability,
     Performance, and
     Supportability (FURPS), 206

G

Garbage collector tool, 168
General-purpose input/output
     (GPIO), 204
Git, 203
   CAD, 1
   clean untracked files, 59, 60
   commands, 2, 60, 61
   commits, 32
   comparing algorithms,
      35–37, 39–43
   definition, 1
   delete file, 14
   get file out of commit, 57, 58
   ignore file, 19, 20, 22
   local repository, 33, 34
   log history, 27, 29–31
   Microsoft Windows, 3, 4, 6
   rename/relocate file, 16–18
   repository, 6–12, 23–27
   reset, 48–50, 52, 53
   restore, 44–47
   revert, 54–57
   stage area, 12, 13
git diff command, 201
GitHub, 147
Graphical user interface (GUI), 2

H, I, J

HEAD pointer, 78, 82, 109

K

KiCad, 232

L

local repository, 4
log command, 33, 74, 166

M, N, O

-m parameter, 72
Mean time between failures
(MTBF), 207

P, Q

Programmable Logic Controller
(PLC) systems, 200
pull command, 146, 157

R

Raspberry Pi (RPi), 203
rebase command, 100, 178, 179
"reflogExpireUnreachable"
parameter, 168
Remote repository
centralized and distributed
repository models, 121
central repository, 122
cloning, 124, 125
connections, 139, 140, 142,
144–146, 148, 162, 163
fork, 160–162
GitHub, 122–124
independent repositories,
merge, 156–158
push/fetch/pull commands,
126–131, 133–138
race condition, 148–151, 153
scaled projects, 159
tags/release, 153–155
reset command, 110

restore command, 116
revert command, 54, 111
rm command, 15
RPi COM 4, extension board
definition, 227
diff command, 228
GitHub issue tracking system, 234
GPIO, 227, 230–232
mergetool, 233

S

show command, 13
Spiral development method, 193
switch command, 67
SyncBox, 159, 203
Altium designer/git, 224–227
BOM, 223
definition, 204, 205, 208, 209
functionality requirements, 207
implementation, 216–223
radiology scanners, 204
radiology technician
registers, 204
reliability, 207
requirement analysis, 205
supportability, 208
system analysis, 209–211
system design, 212, 214, 215
X-ray scanner, 203

T, U, V

Tags, 117, 153

INDEX

W

Waterfall methodology, 194
Workspace, 3

X, Y, Z

X-ray scanner, 203

Printed in the United States
by Baker & Taylor Publisher Services